MASTERS OF WORLD LITERATURE

PUBLISHED:

GEORGE ELIOT *by Walter Allen*
JOHN MILTON *by Douglas Bush*
JONATHAN SWIFT *by Nigel Dennis*
HONORE DE BALZAC *by E. J. Oliver*

IN PREPARATION:

PROUST *by William Barrett*
FLAUBERT *by Jacques Barzun*
COLERIDGE *by W. J. Bate*
KEATS *by Douglas Bush*
SAMUEL JOHNSON *by James L. Clifford*
YEATS *by F. W. Dupee*
JOYCE *by Leon Edel*
D. H. LAWRENCE *by Monroe Engel*
DANTE *by Francis Fergusson*
CONRAD *by Elizabeth Hardwick*
THOREAU *by Granville Hicks*
HARDY *by Irving Howe*
JANE AUSTEN *by Louis Kronenberger*
EMERSON *by Alfred Kazin*
POE *by Dwight Macdonald*
FIELDING *by Midge Podhoretz*
HENRY JAMES *by Richard Poirier*
TOLSTOY *by Philip Rahv*
MELVILLE *by Harold Rosenberg*
BEN JONSON *by Raymond Rosenthal*
WORDSWORTH *by Lionel Trilling*

MASTERS OF WORLD LITERATURE SERIES

LOUIS KRONENBERGER, GENERAL EDITOR

Jonathan Swift

◄((◄((◄((A SHORT CHARACTER))◄))◄))◄

by Nigel Dennis

The Macmillan Company, New York
Collier-Macmillan Limited, London

To
Ernan Forbes-Dennis
with grateful affection

PART ONE

AN IMPORTANT DUTY of the "County Committees" set up by the Roundheads in the English Civil War was that of receiving information about the misdeeds of local Cavaliers and punishing their "malignancy". The members of these Committees often found it difficult to do this work properly, for in the areas that were loyal to the King most of the suppression and punishment was being done to them. In the county of Hereford, for example, that lively "malignant", Sir Henry Lingen, besieged and sacked the castle of Brampton Bryan, whose Puritan landlords, the Harleys, were prominent members of the Herefordshire Committee. And here begins an interesting and romantic story.

After reducing the seat of the Harleys, Sir Henry Lingen marched to the opposite end of the county, by-passing the walled city of Hereford, which the King's men were holding against a sizeable army of Scottish Presbyterians. Lingen seized the abandoned fortress of Goodrich Castle and settled down to fortify and defend it. He did this work so well that Goodrich was the last stronghold in England to hold out for the King. When it was captured at last, in 1646, after Hereford had fallen to the Scots, the "malignant" defenders were marched off to prison in Raglan Castle and the prominent among them received their appropriate punishments.

One of these prominent "malignants" was the Reverend Thomas Swift, Vicar of Goodrich. This doughty, romantic priest was the sort of man whose real deeds are exciting enough to inspire legendary ones and whose evil in the eyes of his enemies is exactly proportionate to his glory in the eyes of his friends. In the month that Goodrich fell, Swift was ejected from his benefice by the County Committee "on information of his scandalous life", and though it is impossible to describe either his deeds or his suffering with accuracy, one can put together a pretty judicious combination of facts and legends.

Swift's father and his father's father were both men of Kent and both vicars of St. Andrews, Canterbury: Thomas Swift seems to have come to Goodrich because he inherited a small estate there from his mother. His wife was a Dryden, a near relation of the poet. They had at least eleven children, most of whom were born by 1636, when the Vicar built "New House", a pretty little stone manor-cum-vicarage shaped like the letter Y, on the porch of which the date of building and the Vicar's initials may be seen to this day.

The Vicar's "scandalous life" began with the beginnings of the Civil War. An informer told the County Committee that from the pulpit of Ross Church Swift had preached vehemently in support of the King, taking as his text "Render unto Caesar the things which are Caesar's". When the King raised levies in Monmouthshire, the Vicar was said to have "bought armes and conveyed them into Monmouthshire": he denied this charge. By 1642 he was deemed "malignant" enough to receive punishment, and New House was sacked by Roundhead soldiers. We are told by a furious partisan that this was the first of "more than thirty spoliations", in the course of which the Vicar was robbed of "all his provisions of Victualls, Corne, Household-stuffe", his horses and his carts, "all Iron, Pewter, and Brasse", all his clothing and his children's clothing; indeed, the very bowl from which his infant child was eating porridge. His cattle, it is said, he attempted to hide in the big cellars, which opened onto the surrounding fields; but all such evasions were useless, and New House was plundered entirely. It is easy to imagine what it looked like afterwards, for we have only to visit it today— dilapidated, neglected and surrounded by the squalid sheds of its poor tenants—to get a good idea of what a plundered home looks like.

The Vicar had fled into hiding, but only in order to work more mischief. In 1644, we are told, he strewed the ford across the Wye at Goodrich with caltrops, a sort of spiked iron balls very harmful to cavalry: legend has it that he was "of a mechanick turn" and forged the caltrops with his own hands. Legend also assures us that the Roundheads lost no less than two hundred horsemen, drowned or killed, as a result. Meanwhile, the Vicar had mortgaged his small estate, and when Charles fled to Raglan Castle after the Battle of Naseby, Swift marched to the castle and asked to see him. On being asked why, he replied: "I am come to give him my coat"; and on being told that something more substantial was required at this stage, answered: "Then he shall have my waist-coat too". He then took off this garment and sent it in to the King: inside its seams were "three hundred broad pieces of gold".

It is not certain that the Reverend Thomas Swift was one of the garrison of Goodrich Castle, but it is possible that he was, because he was marched off to the same prison as the defenders immediately after the surrender. We know certainly that he returned to his ruined home and estate without benefice or prebend and with a fine of £300 against him. Of his subsequent battles with the Herefordshire County Committee we also know very little; though there is no doubt that he fought for himself vigorously and that some of his letters, once thought to have been "preserved among the papers of Sir Edward Harley", are still in existence. Under the Commonwealth he lived the life of a renegade High Church outlaw, and though he retained the bare bones of his small estate, he was never restored to his living nor to any sort of prosperity. That is why five of his sons, when the Restoration came, hurried over to Ireland to recoup the family fortunes. But the Vicar never lived to see this: he died in the same year as Oliver Cromwell, four years before the king came back.

✥((✥((✥((●   ))✥))✥))✥

Brampton Bryan passed through Sir Edward Harley to his son Robert, 1st Earl of Oxford and Mortimer: when this great man became Queen Anne's first minister of state, he chose as spokesman for his party the Vicar of Goodrich's grandson, Jonathan Swift. New House passed to the Vicar's eldest son, Godwin, and through Godwin and his son after him to Deane Swift, who was the first editor of the *Journal to Stella*. But as far as we know, Jonathan Swift never visited New House until 1727, when he was Dean of St. Patrick's and in his sixtieth year: his purpose in coming to Goodrich was to set up a suitable memorial to his grandfather's memory.

In this he was setting a good example. Memorials to the great dead were much on his mind at that time, for he believed that his contemporaries, including his own relations, were an avaricious, degenerate lot who had quite lost the love of honour and liberty that had inspired their grandfathers. For some time he had taken pleasure in examining the memorials in St. Patrick's Cathedral, deciding which ones were in a state of decay, and which ones were not there at all, much as they deserved to be. Letters, signed by himself and his Chapter, had been going out for some time to the descendants of these worthy ancestors: they were requested politely either to renovate their forebears' monuments or to erect the missing ones: in the event of their failing to do so, they were told, the Dean and Chapter would do the job instead at the expense of the Cathedral and would feel bound to state in the engraved inscription that such action had been made necessary by the parsimony and ingratitude of the descendants. Some of the lords and ladies who received these awful letters dispatched the necessary money with all haste; the rest paid no attention and received, carved imperishably in Latin, a lasting monument to their neglectful beastliness. Memorially speaking, Swift's greatest trophy was to be the head of George II, when the King ignored the demand for a monument to the Duke of Schomberg, who had died fighting for England at the Battle of the Boyne. By 1731 the Schomberg monument was in place, with the customary penalty clause engraved upon it, and the King's indignant shout, "Damn Dr. Swift!" had been reported to the Dean and accepted with high pleasure.

Now, at New House, Swift ordered a tablet to be set up in Goodrich Church and wrote the inscription for it: if this tablet ever went up, it has not survived, which is a great pity, because Swift's tablets make good reading. The Dean also presented the Church with the small, silver chalice out of which, it is thought, his grandfather had continued secretly to serve his communicants after his ejection: on the base of this he wrote in Latin: "Thomas Swift, Vicar of this Church, well known in history for what he performed and suffered under King Charles 1., administered out of this same chalice."; and he added that the present was the gift of the Cavalier's grandson, Dean of St. Patrick's in Dublin. This chalice is Goodrich Church's proudest possession to this day, and though, designed as it was for surreptitious communication, it is impractical to use and spends most of its time in the bank, it is brought out proudly on feast days.

Having made these obeisances to his ancestor and honoured the spirit of the place with a large order for cider, the Dean passed on to London. He showed his friend Pope his inscription for the tablet, discussed the design of it with him, and got so impassioned and garrulous on the subjects of his grandfather and Goodrich that his friend began to smile and, shortly, scribbled down what he suggested might be a better inscription for the tablet:

> Jonathan Swift
> Had the gift
> By fatheridge, motheridge
> And by brotheridge
> To come down from Gutheridge.
> But now is spoil'd clean
> And an Irish Dean.
> In this church he has put
> A stone of two foot
> With a cup and a can, sir,
> In respect of his grandsire.
> So, Ireland, change thy tone
> And cry: O hone, O hone,
> For England has its own.

*   *   *

Elderly men do not pay such tributes to their grandsires as a rule; when they do, it is because of the promptings of some sort of emotion. Middleton Murry thinks that in Swift's case the emotion was a feeling of homelessness, heightened by the recent death of Hester Johnson: Swift went to Goodrich to attach himself to a strong family root, and also, as Pope's rhyme suggests, to assert his right to be regarded as English, not Irish. But there are other reasons why Swift was drawn to his grandfather's place, and to understand them we must study the effect of Thomas Swift's life and fate upon his descendants.

The most immediate effect was to make struggling immigrants of a family of gentry—"a family not undistinguished in its time", as Swift put it. Five of Thomas Swift's sons went to Ireland, and thanks to the marriage of the eldest, Godwin, to a relation of the greatest man in Ireland, the Duke of Ormond, four of the sons established themselves well. The fifth, and youngest, Jonathan, had no time to get on his feet: he died when he was only twenty-five. But he was a married man and left two children behind, a daughter named Jane and a son, Jonathan, who was born about seven months after his father's death.

Swift tells us clearly how much his father's marriage and decease affected his life. The marriage, entered into by a poor younger son before he was financially established, and then dissolved by sudden death, had consequences which, Swift says, he was to feel "throughout the whole course of his life". It caused the widow to return to her home in England, to exist on a pittance, and it caused the son to grow up without mother or father, dependent on the charity of his uncles. Swift received the best education that Ireland could give, going to Kilkenny School (an Ormond establishment) at the age of six, and to Trinity College, Dublin, at fourteen. But though we may argue that such an upbringing was adequate and generous, our opinion in the matter is of no importance: the only interest is in how it was regarded by the beneficiary, because it is his conclusions, and not ours, that helped to shape his views and character. Swift thought he was treated disgracefully, and to what he called "the ill-treatment of his nearest relations" he attributed the fact that when he got to Trinity College "he was so discouraged and sunk in his spirits that he too much neglected his academic studies", was "stopped of his degree for dulness and insufficiency; and at last hardly admitted in a manner little to his credit. . . ." It has been suggested that he did better at university than he supposed; but here, again, it is only Swift's opinion that matters: we come too late to reassure him.

There is not a great deal of information about these first twenty years of Swift's life, so we should pay particular attention to what Swift tells us about them. We should not be put off by the fact that Swift's recollections are not always accurate, because what he recollects is probably more accurate and certainly more pertinent than what we invent. He tells us clearly, for instance, of a boyhood of frustration and disappointment, describing his struggles as those of "a younger son of younger sons". This description is not strictly accurate; probably it is a misquotation from Shakespeare*, but we know perfectly well what Swift means by it. Nor is there any reason to doubt him when he writes: "I remember when I was a little boy, I felt a great fish at the end of my line which I drew up almost on the ground, but it dropt in, and the disappointment vexeth me to this very day, and I believe it was the type of all my future disappointments". It was. And to this recollection Sheridan adds an anecdote that is an exact psychological parallel: he tells us that

* *Henry IV, Part I*, Act 4, Scene 2: ". . . discarded unjust serving men, younger sons to younger brothers, revolted tapsters . . ." Swift's lack of interest in Shakespeare is taken for granted, particularly as none of Shakespeare's works was to be found in Swift's library at the end of his life. But his correspondence suggests considerable interest in Shakespeare, though he centered it, as we would expect, on the Histories.

In 1704 and 1718 he quotes from *Henry V*, choosing on each occasion the same Act and Scene (IV, 7) and the same character, Fluellen: one can see that the Welsh captain's murdering of the English language would amuse Swift, but perhaps it is worth remarking, too, that the scene in question has ardent references to the Swift family territory of the Wye Valley. In 1712, in the *Journal to Stella*, Swift compares himself to the fallen Wolsey and misquotes the two famous lines from *Henry VIII* describing Wolsey's begging shelter of the Abbot of Leicester. In a letter of 1715 he returns again to Wolsey and *Henry VIII*. Henry VI's soliloquy on the quiet hillside during the Battle of Tawton, in *Henry VI, Part III*, Act 2, Scene 5, obtains a reference in a letter when Swift was a schoolboy he saw an old horse on its way to the knackers and bought it for eighteen pence, to enjoy the glory of riding high and mighty through Kilkenny. But no sooner had he mounted it than the poor beast dropped dead.

The important thing to note is the effect upon Swift of 'his struggles and disappointments. We know that they were humiliating, long-lasting, and temporarily discouraging, but we know, too, that he was not diverted by them from his principal aim in life. What that aim was, he tells us exactly, in a letter to Pope:

> I am ashamed to tell you, that when I was very young I had more desire to be famous than ever since. . . . . I will further tell you that all my endeavours, from a boy, to distinguish myself, were only for want of a great title and fortune, that I might be used like a Lord by those who have an opinion of my parts—whether right or wrong, it is no great matter, and so the reputation of wit or great learning does the office of a blue ribbon, or of a coach and six horses.

If we rest upon this rock, we are pretty safe. If an old man tells us that all his endeavours since boyhood were to heal the sick and make the world a kinder place, we may suspect that the passage of years has tilted his

---

of 1713, and one may note that the idea of retiring from worldly struggle to a rustic hilltop occurs repeatedly in Swift's letters in moments of hermitic despondency. As to the other plays of Shakespeare, there is a paraphrase of lines from *Antony and Cleopatra* in *A Tale of a Tub* and from *"Mackbeth"* in a poem of 1731. In 1721 Swift wrote an epilogue to *Hamlet* for a charity performance. It is probable that he knew *Julius Caesar*; it is possible that he knew *A Winter's Tale*.

If so much familiarity with Shakespeare can be gleaned merely from passing references and paraphrases, there is no saying how much more may have actually existed. As an act of pure guesswork, one might hazard that Swift read in his youth, but eschewed later, the romantic tragedies and comedies, but always remained attached to the plays that satisfied his liking for the combination of poetry and history.

No consideration has been given here to the admiration of Shakespeare expressed in *A Letter to a Young Poet*, because this work shows no sign of having been written by Swift.

memory a little; but if "a younger son of younger sons" confesses to a boyhood determination to rise high in the world through his wits and be "used like a Lord", we may accept the statement as true, particularly if we know that the course of his life followed this particular ambition with immense success. The frank avowal also tells us where the energy, pride and determination came from and why even small slights and petty humiliations roused such anger in one who was determined to be "used like a Lord". Moreover, Swift's is an ambition that we recognize immediately; it is the response to fallen dignity that occurs repeatedly in the stories of literary men; it is the condition of Trollope, Dickens and Shaw, who showed, as Swift did, that the final product need not be at all demeaned by the initial inspiration. In Swift's case the grandfather's fall was to be the grandson's stimulus, and the strength and resolution that is inspired by such a fallen status is well expressed by Middleton through the mouth of De Flores:

> Though my hard fate has thrust me out to servitude,
> I tumbled into th' world a gentleman.
> She turns her blessed eye upon me now,
> And I'll endure all storms before I part with 't.

*   *   *

The second major effect of Thomas Swift's life upon his grandson runs parallel with the first, in that the enemies who were responsible for the family's fallen status became the principal demons of the grandson's life and the foremost target of his satire. For when the Cavalier's sons immigrated into Ireland they found it swarming with the very monsters that had been their father's ruin. We think of Ireland as a Roman Catholic country, so we find it difficult to imagine that in the 1660's the eastern seaboard and the North were established provinces of Dissent and Presbyterianism, and more so at the Restoration than at any former time, thanks to Cromwell's large Puritan settlements and colonies. The Church of Swift's grandfather had both position and magnitude in Ireland, but it was a harried, discomfited establishment, declined in its fortunes and dependent upon official English support if it was to hold its own against the Nonconfórmist majority. Often, this support was not given, for the plain, political reason that a colony that is loyal to the mother country on one principle should not be pushed into discontent by the strong imposition of a different principle; unless, of course, some money is at stake. Moreover, in Ireland's case, Nonconformity and Presbyterianism were a much stronger check than the Church of Ireland to the Catholicism of the natives, as the Ulstermen proved when they rose for King William at the Boyne. Thus religion was politics, and politics was religion; and the denominations *Whig* and *Tory* were as much religious as political. Any study of Swift's views must stress this fact above all others, because he was one to whom politics was always religion and to whom the only quarrel between Whig and Tory was that which concerned the treatment of Nonconformists. Swift believed all his life that they should be denied every possible privilege—which made him a High Tory in practice. Yet he insisted to his dying day that he was a Whig—in that he accepted the legality of King William. He thought there was nothing contradictory in these separate assumptions. Nor, indeed, was there, but for the fact that the meanings of names change with the times. The "old Whiggish principles" which Swift upheld were not the principles of the Whig party in his lifetime. The living Whig placated the Dissenters: he needed their votes. But Swift would have denied them the right to vote at all.

We may assume that this view of Swift's derived partly from the downfall of his family and partly from the situation into which this downfall pushed them. One

important consequence of the view was Swift's irremedi-
able religious phobia—his determination to see the devil
wholly in Dissent and hardly at all in Roman Catholicism. The Papists receive a fair share of his satire in
A Tale of a Tub and win occasional obnoxious references
in his other writings, but they are never at any time
regarded as a danger to the Church or even as an enemy
to the nation.

The question of Popery, Swift insists, is one that has
been disposed of entirely and is no longer a suitable
topic for serious political discussion: it must be left to
the howling rabble and lunatic churchmen, who inflame
one another with cries of "No Popery!" The man who
walks in fear of Popery, Swift says, distracts himself from
noticing the everlasting perils of Dissent; indeed, most
of what is blamed upon Popery, Swift argues, is merely
a cunning invention of Dissent. He is unmoved by the
fact that he himself was obliged to flee from Trinity
College and take refuge in England when James II
invaded Ireland and set up his parliament in Dublin: he
is equally unmoved by the fact that the Irish Papists rose
in murderous rebellion during the English Civil War:
the villains, to him, are still Cromwell and his Puritans,
who supplied them with the opportunity—"who tied our
hands, while the Papists cut our throats". "We regard
them as no more dangerous than their women and children", he wrote firmly in an early pamphlet; and in his
years of political greatness he never ceased to make
mock of those who were foolish enough to believe that
his Tory friends inclined to Jacobitism. Dissent was the
only treason he was prepared to see, and the realm could
be invaded only by Scotsmen. The history of his family
was the history of the kingdom.

✻   ✻   ✻

But was it really his family? From his own lifetime to
the present day, biographers have argued that it was not.

They have found something fishy in Swift's account of his childhood and have felt that it cannot explain properly the relative ease with which he seems to have passed from early obscurity in Ireland to prominence in England. His birth, seven months after his father's death, has looked suspicious. His extraordinary story of having then been kidnapped by his English nurse and carried across the sea by her to Cumberland, where he spent his first four years, has seemed much too fanciful to be acceptable. For these reasons, many biographers have supported the suggestion that he was the illegitimate son of his first patron, Sir William Temple, or of Sir William Temple's father, Sir John. This, they say, would explain his having received such a good education and having been introduced to Court society by Temple when he came of age.

This explanation may be perfectly correct. The only thing about it that is open to criticism is the fact that it is unimportant.

It is unimportant because, as has been seen, Swift passed his whole life in the belief that he was the legitimate son of Jonathan and the legitimate grandson of Thomas. His views on politics and religion grew up in the light of this belief; his ambition was rooted in it; his pilgrimage to Goodrich was made in honour of a forebear whom he believed implicitly to be such. If he was, in truth, illegitimate, the fact escaped his attention. If his genetic composition was not what he supposed it to be, his outlook was not twisted or afflicted by that of which he was ignorant. What we may call the slant of his life—its prevailing prejudice, or chief signpost—is the line that carries him back to Goodrich. And what we may call the burden of his chief complaint against the world is his conviction that the days of his grandfather's prime were days from which his own times had degenerated. For Swift is not a man who looks to the future hopefully and tries to persuade others to "advance". He is one

who tries to push the world back to an earlier condition.
The monuments he struggles to raise and to repair are
not sentimental whims. They represent the direction in
which he tried to push his own life and the ideals to
which he aspired. Those ideals never varied, so far as one
can tell, from the beginning of his life to the end of it. He
tells us frequently and exactly what they were, and if we
set them out before us and study them we are able to
see very clearly the position that Swift allotted to himself
and his contemporaries in the history of civilization. This
"history" is one which he has culled from his reading,
and upon it he bases the major principles of his own life.

He has read the Greek philosophers and found them
good—so good that he carries a knife to thrust into the
clergymen who scorn such "Heathen religions". He will
sharply remind a young clergyman that the ideal of
brotherly love is to be found in Socrates before it is pro-
claimed by Christ, and he is moved almost to brotherly
hate when he hears an ignorant preacher denounce those
"good men" of antiquity. Why, then, is he himself a
Christian clergyman and not a heathen philosopher?

He answers this shortly and clearly, in an argument
that we understand very well today because we are still
hearing it: an ideal, he says, no matter how elevated it
may be, must have the sanction of divine authority
if it is to be stable and unarguable. The Will of God is,
therefore, the source of all authority, and no authority
can be real without it. History, Swift believes, confirms
this hypothesis, for history tells us that the Greek sages,
having no Omnipotence above them, fell into furious
wrangles and disputes, thus demonstrating the inade-
quacy of earthly wisdom and giving proof that faction
(the most awful of words, to Swift) is the inevitable
outcome of all debate upon fundamentals.

From the essential Will proceeds the essential Word,
insofar as this has been vouchsafed to man. This Word
is in the Gospels; therefore, it is of vital importance that

there be no tampering with and embellishing of the "plain English" of the Gospels: this, as we know, is the absolute foundation on which the wild fancy of *A Tale of a Tub* is built. For no sooner is God's plain Word revealed to man than man responds by editing and distorting it, and once this happens, the authority of the Word is weakened and unity in God becomes faction in man. Swift shows how intensely he believes this when he suggests that even St. Paul's tongue was not entirely under control: just as Johnson thought Swift was not a safe example, so did Swift think that the Pauline style had a bad effect on lesser men. "I have been often offended to find St. Paul's allegories, and other figures of Grecian eloquence, converted by divines into articles of faith", he writes. "I may venture to insist further", he says elsewhere, "that many terms used in Holy Writ, particularly by St. Paul, might with more Discretion be changed into plainer Speech, except when they are introduced as part of a quotation".

The caricaturing of God begins almost at the moment at which God reveals his Image: man's first response to revealed truth is to try to make it look bigger, better and gaudier. Grecian eloquence is the first of the silver buttons that the brothers in *A Tale of a Tub* affix to their homespun cloaks; for silver buttons are the fashion of their day as "Grecian" thought was the fashion of the Alexandrian intellectuals. Fashion and snobbery work together to turn even the Early Fathers from the simple truth: they embellish the Word because they are ashamed of its simplicity and because they feel the need to raise the Word onto a more intellectual base—to make it *arguable*. And in this matter Swift is adamant: he will allow not a single word of argument about the revealed word. Argument in such a matter is not only blasphemous but a denial of authority itself: it is the mark of insolence and stupidity in the clergyman.

Here, again, we see his anger rise, as he denounces

those "too numerous" clerics who are so misguided as to try to explain the inexplicable. What words can describe the pride and insolence of the "Broad", or "Rational", Churchman, who, in effect, denies God's right to propound a mystery and takes upon himself the duty of "explaining" it? Or, as we might put it: which is the more religious clergyman—the one who confines himself to his human privileges and defends God's word in *A Tale of a Tub* or the one who assumes divine authority and explains to man that which God forbore to explain? We will only say that the latter has the better chance of being made a bishop.

Swift's faith is built on this rock, and from it fan out all his views on all subjects—his hatred of paint and powder, his scorn for embellishment, his diatribes against contrived conversation and the dictates of fashion. His is by no means an unique point of view, but it is the starting point of his satire and the solid ground out of which his fantasy grows into its extraordinary shapes. How closely and vigorously he hewed to his rule of the unmodified Word we may see from his sermons: they show his strength, his immense precision and his strong passions, but they emit hardly a breath of his fabulous spirit and are severely unadorned in respect of wit and fancy. This has led to the suggestion that the sermon was not Swift's forte: we would propose, instead, that Swift's sermons show exactly the strong line he drew between religion and fiction. Had he wanted his sermons to sound extraordinary, there is no doubt that they would have sounded very extraordinary indeed.

Let us now follow the authority of the Word, as Swift himself followed it, up through the centuries until we reach his own day. The human intellect, dragging its wriggling convolutions into the Gospel like the serpent into Paradise, or a sophisticated beau into decent society, corrupts the Word and makes man his own authority. The Arians question the divinity of Christ: in opposition to them, St. Athanasius endeavours with "zeal and courage" to explain the mystery of the Holy Trinity. But this Mystery cannot be explained, be the saint never so wise; and so the Authority of the Word is weakened by saint as well as sinner. The Christians, then, become no better than the factious Greek philosophers; what is more, as the centuries pass, they turn precisely to these unauthorized heathens for help in their factional disputes—"which hath since occasioned very pernicious consequences, stopt the progress of Christianity, and been a great promoter of vice. . . ."

The "glorious Reformation" does much to restore the power of the Word, stripping the reformed faith of numerous man-made terms such as *Indulgences* and *Purgatory*. But in place of Authority, it brings in an iniquitous man-trap named *Liberty of Conscience*. What is this so-called *Liberty*? It is, as Swift sees it, one of those terms that must fail for want of control. Epicurus made clear to himself and his disciples that in advancing pleasure as the end of man, he did so because he deemed virtue the highest pleasure; but he was no more able to confine pleasure within this virtuous frame than the Reformers were able to confine "Liberty of Conscience" within the frame of a stable religion: the cat got out of the bag. That a man's conscience must have liberty, Swift does not deny, for he says drily that "To say a man is bound to believe, is neither true nor sense", and adds: "You may force men, by interest or punishment, to say or swear they believe, and to act as if they believed: You can go no further". But he insists adamantly that where a man's belief conflicts with the belief of an established Church, that man may enjoy the liberty of his belief only on condition that he hold his tongue and be "content with the possession of his own opinion in private"; he sums this up in a smart phrase: "particular men should be quiet".

Thus liberty of conscience may exist in man's mind

and heart but must never be translated into public action; for if it is, the one Word is shattered into numerous words and the one Truth into multiple human truths. "Violent zeal for truth", says Swift, "hath an hundred to one odds to be either petulancy, ambition, or pride"—and we may note that it is these glosses, these marginal notes, that give perspicacity to his orthodoxy. Many divines may have preached the principles we have set down here, but only Swift could sauce them with the little extras:

God's mercy is over all his works, but divines of all sorts lessen that mercy too much.

*　*　*

When the plain Word has been corrupted and over-laid with human fancies, good churchmen have the right to rebel against the Established Church because it no longer represents the original authority and is thus no longer authority at all. Swift, therefore, is not only con-tent to reject Rome but to dismiss it as an issue long since settled and done with: his concern is with what the Reformers did to the Word once they had restored it to primacy. Poor Word! It was restored to England under the aegis of Henry VIII, a king whom Swift de-tests above all kings: "He was only an Instrument of [Reformation] (as the logicians speak) by accident; nor doth he appear throughout his whole Reign, to have had any other Views, than those of gratifying his insatiable Love of Power, Cruelty, Oppression, and other irregular Appetites. . . . Neither has any Thing disgusted me more in reading the Histories of those Times, than to see one of the worst Princes of any Age or Country, celebrated as an instrument in that glorious work of the Refor-mation".

Under Henry VIII the churchly representatives of the restored Word are plundered, robbed and reduced to ignominy. Into this weakened castle march the Anabap-tists and Puritans, and thus the Word is assailed by the impious rich and royal on the one hand and the Dissenting rabble on the other. "Those wicked Puritans began, in Queen Elizabeth's time, to quarrel only with surplices . . . with the ring in matrimony, the cross in baptism, and the like"; but as the years passed: "In their self will they digged down a wall". Yet there was one brief moment when the wall stood as Swift desired a wall to stand: this was the reign of Charles I.

What this reign meant to Swift is of first importance in understanding him—for it meant everything; it was as much the Golden Age to him as the days of Marathon were to Aristophanes and the days of the Republic to Juvenal. Most satirists are conservative men, and almost all of them are conservative because they have a powerful conviction that *times were better once*. Under Charles the Martyr, as Swift saw that reign, England reached something like perfection. The Word stood plain to see; the fanatic Dissenters were penalized by Laud, in England, and by Strafford, in Ireland. Manners and customs, purified of the extravagances and romanticisms of cruder times, reached a civilized niceness they had never known before. Women were admitted to court—a huge step forward—and the conversation they participated in there was always about intelligent and thoughtful matters, never vulgar and brutish. The English language climbed from barbarism to near perfection: as seen through Swift's eyes, it did so in a peculiar jump from Spenser and Sidney to Charles himself ("a great patron of learning"); and what it underwent for good or bad under Shakespeare and his contemporaries, Swift tells us nothing, for though he read Shakespeare, the period was not one that he esteemed.

When "That murderous Puritan-parliament" rose against their king, all this glory departed, and the world "changed every day from schism to schism, from heresy to heresy, and from one faction to another". The ideal of pure, stalwart friendship which Swift valued so highly—

the ideal which marked his grandfather's bond with
Charles and his own with Harley and St. John—had
already been inexcusably smirched when the execution
of his friend Strafford was forced upon Charles by "the
tumult and threatenings of the packed rabble". Charles's
martyrdom was virtually the end of all good things; from
that date forth, "rebellion and murder," atheism and free-
thought, became commonplace corruptions of English
life. Moreover, the history of the so-called Protectorate
repeated exactly the most evil moments in the histories
of Greece and Rome: lawful authority, overthrown by a
factious rabble, must be replaced by an authority that
will bring the rabble under control again, and this new
authority is invariably a despot. What Caesar was to the
divided Romans, Cromwell was to the quarrelling Puritans—a necessary consequence of the initial treason. Thus,
to kill a king in the name of liberty is to obtain despotism
in the name of a Lord Protector.

The Restoration could not check the "numberless
villainies" that the Protectorate had introduced, because
Charles II was too indolent and "dissipated" and James II
was "seduced to Popery". Under good King William a
little of the old good returned—"God gave him greater
success than our sins deserved. But, as a house thrown
down by a storm is seldom rebuilt, without some change
in the foundation, so it hath happened, that, since the
late Revolution, men have sate much looser in the true
fundamentals of both religion and government, and fac-
tions have been more violent, treacherous, and malicious
than ever. . . ." Belief in a single authority has been
replaced by a detestable individualism that Swift describes in another admirable phrase: "Every man his own
Carver".

＊　　＊　　＊

We shall not dispute at all Swift's view of history,
ancient or modern; our sole interest is to find out what
fundamentals he sat in, what lessons he derived from his

reading of "history" and how these lessons affected the course of his life.

There are two principal ones, and these dovetail exactly with his own principles and with the history of his own family. The first is that "Particular men", those who carve for themselves, are innately vicious men, because though they may claim that "truth" is their ideal and "liberty" their aim, they are ruled in fact by pride, ambition and greed, and their intention, finally, is to undermine truth and destroy liberty. When Milton demands greater freedom of divorce, he does so with a show of honesty; but the hard fact behind the apparent honesty is that Milton himself has married a "shrew" and is pressing upon others a reform for which he pines himself. He could as well, Swift suggests cruelly, once blind, have pressed upon mankind the necessity for a general blindness and put up some fine arguments to prove that a total lack of vision would be of the highest benefit to the commonwealth. So the wise man must always look for the selfish motive behind the projected reform and judge of the proposed "liberty" by an examination of the man who proposes it. Thus, one might say, if Pope and Defoe were to propose the same reform, it would be good when it came from Pope, because Pope is a virtuous man, but bad when it came from Defoe, because a Dissenter cannot but have a vicious aim in view. It is this peculiar line of argument that proves, in effect, that Defoe is bound to be more malicious than Pope, and it is why the former is dismissed as "that rogue that was stood in the pillory" although the latter is assured of a good *entrée* into heaven. Pope, it should be noted, must also be regarded as the more trustworthy *because* he is a Roman Catholic: his may not be the perfect religious state, but it is one which rates a real stability far above a vicious individualism and exemplifies the truth that "all wise Christian governments . . . always had some established religion, leaving at best a toleration to others". Swift believed this so ardently that it obliged him even to tip his hat, though only briefly, to that monster-wrecker, Oliver Cromwell. For when the Irish Papists begged Cromwell to concede them their religious liberty the despot was shrewd enough to answer that they might be as free as they pleased—provided they refrained from preaching, held no masses and burnt no candles.

Thus the second major lesson of history is the necessity for a single joint authority, ecclesiastical and political. And because Swift urges us to look closely at the motives of a man who has something to propose, let us take his advice and ask what were *his* motives in disliking tolerance and making authority the absolute backbone of his morality?

The blunt answer is that he loved authority more dearly than anything else. How far this was due to the lowered status that the collapse of authority had brought upon him and his family, we cannot say; but we can say surely that he desired dignity inordinately and regarded dignity and authority as two elements that stood or fell together. Authority stood so high in his regard that he had small respect for kings: this is not a paradox; it means simply that he despised kings because they took so frivolous or brutish a view of the nature of authority: they betrayed the dignity of great office. Swift expected them to do so: he liked to point out that the education of a young king consisted largely of lies, flattery and chicanery and that only the rare monarch could be expected to survive his disgusting childhood. But the lesson he drew from this was that a people should rally to their king like social workers rallying to a delinquent. For authority lay in this poor creature, and he should be disclaimed or attacked only if his natural abominableness became intolerable. Swift's view of kings is no better than Shelley's and Byron's; but Swift, unlike these later poets, was tolerant of kings because he cherished, rather than detested, authority.

What he cherished in kings he cherished equally in himself. To be "used like a Lord" was no figure of speech: it was an absolute imperative. Those who used him otherwise, or led him into courses that proved injurious to his dignity, aroused in him instantly the fury of a king of the beasts. No friendship, however old, survived a suspicion on Swift's part that it had rendered him undignified, nor was there ever forgiveness for those who disdained his virtues or failed to recognize his services. His contempt for the Irish people was limitless, but when kings, ministers and high-born friends left him in the lurch he became the leader of the very rabble he most despised. He did not fight for their liberties because he loved them but because they were absolutely obedient to his commands. The people's liberty was the Dean's authority.

❀   ❀   ❀

It is easy to see why Ireland was the worst place in the world for the nativity of such a man. To the end of his days Swift denied that he was one of "this land of slaves": he was "dropped" in Dublin, he said, by "accident". Even the thought of being dead in Ireland was so repugnant to him that only at the end of his life did he remove from his will the clause that ordered that his dead body be carried to England and buried at Holyhead. His friends knew his feelings in this matter and took infinite care to treat him as an Englishman: Pope would speak to him of England as "your native land". But those who disliked or distrusted him had no such tact, and Swift's preferment to the Deanery of St. Patrick's was not only a dismissal into exile but a horrible affront to his pride.

His quarrel with Ireland was entirely one of dignity. The man who was born a Scotsman and made himself a vile nuisance in religion and politics was rewarded for his unceasing malice with an Act of Union and a policy of toleration. But the man who was born in Ireland was

treated like a cur no matter how admirably he behaved—
and before long he responded like a cur, fawning on
those that kicked him. Such a degrading spectacle was
repugnant to Swift, and even while he reviled the man
with the boot, he despised the dog that let himself be
kicked and was disgusted to think that he himself might
be thought a dog of the same breed. Moreover, the dog
was more often than not a dog indeed, descended from
"the sourest leven of Cromwell's army" and a menace to
the Church of Ireland. As a schoolboy, Swift heard these
creatures "crying in the streets for liberty", and as a man
he had no doubt as to what this liberty would mean to
persons such as himself. Once the Nonconformist had
been given his "liberty", he would use it exactly as his
forefathers in England had done—to deny liberty to those
who had been foolish enough to grant it to him. For out
of liberty would come faction, and when faction had
grown intolerable even to itself it would breed a dictator-
ship like Cromwell's, under which Anglicans such as
Swift would suffer precisely the fate of their English
forebears.

And so it is that history becomes, in Swift's eyes, a
gloss on his own family's, and his grandfather's fate
a clear warning of what may be his own. This entirely
personal reading of history is almost invariably disguised
by the simple method of pretending that there is no
such person as Jonathan Swift: there is only a pseudonym
that pretends to be speaking for another self—"Isaac
Bickerstaff", "Lemuel Gulliver", "M. B. Drapier", and so
forth. To play this game properly, the true author must
never interrupt the pretended one; the "I" that is Jonathan
Swift must never make a sudden personal appearance in
territory that has been given to one of his pseudonyms.
Swift soon became so good at playing this game according to the rules that he never, under any circumstances,
let "I" burst through and show the real self behind the
assumed one. That happens only in the first pamphlet

he ever wrote on behalf of Ireland: *A Letter from a Member of the House of Commons in Ireland to a Member of the House of Commons in England Concerning the Sacramental Test (1708).* This protest against granting more privileges to Irish Dissenters lies so close to the author's heart that he cannot keep up the pretence of being a "Member of the House of Commons in Ireland": the mask becomes unhitched when he speaks of Cowley's poems, the mistreatment of Ireland, and recollections of Dissenters "crying out for liberty in the streets". And it falls off completely, revealing Swift himself entirely, when the threat of new privileges for the Dissenters recalls the bitter wrong done to his family:

"Because, methinks, I should be loathe to see my poor titular Bishop *in partibus,* seized on by mistake in the Dark for a Jesuit, or be forced my self to keep a Chaplain disguised like my Butler, and steal to Prayers in a back Room, as my Grandfather used in those Times when the Church of *England* was *malignant*"*.

The personal passion that Swift brings to historical matters extends to all the public attitudes and activities of his life. It is the driving power in his hatred of the Scots, his contempt for the liberal Whigs, his vigorous attacks on Marlborough, who, when he asked that his rank as "Captain General" be granted him for life, "proved" exactly what Swift suspected—that Marlborough, with the help of the Dissenters, meant to make himself a second Cromwell. Moreover, though many ask why Swift became a clergyman, and many more wonder if he was a sincere one, one has only to read his writings and study their principal themes to see that he could hardly have become anything else. "I am inclined to think", says Orrery, "that he entered into orders, more from some private and fixed resolution, than from absolute choice": that this resolution was essentially militant

* The bishop *"in partibus"* is George Coke, Bishop of Hereford, who was ejected from office by the Roundheads.

is shown when Swift speaks of himself as one "sent by Providence to be a clergyman". This remark is notable because it is not characteristic of his general religious attitude. Swift did not usually speak of "Providence" in this intimately "Puritanical" way: the God he believed in was an omniscient authority, not One whose missionary activities were open to description by human beings, still less One who needed the help of clergymen. Where John Donne says ". . . yet I am His creature still, and contribute something to His glory, even in my damnation . . ." Swift only exclaims passionately: "Miserable mortals! can we contribute to *the honour and glory of God?* I could wish that expression were struck out of our Prayer books". Obedience to God is the only duty of man: to insist upon it is the first duty of Swift.

Here is a most interesting kind of general militancy that grows out of adherence to a particular moment of history and, from that same moment, derives its principles, its ambitions, its pugnacity, its ideal of human and personal dignity. We are bound to be impressed by the immense strength of will-power that forces these various tendencies into unity—an individual will that obliges all human history and religion itself to conform absolutely to a personal interpretation of them. Such a will, imposing such a unity, declares both its greatness and its weakness: nothing short of death can stop it, but life cannot fail to balk and punish it because neither the present nor the past can tally with such a wilful bias. So it is that those who are appalled by Swift's vigorous militancy have always the consolation of knowing that it was politically and religiously fruitless and futile; whereas those who cherish above all the immense singularity of his character incline rather to mourn the awful disappointments that it was bound to suffer.

We note of this same unity another interesting thing: it collects together under a head of general indignation both the largest and the smallest elements of human misbehaviour. Proportion seems to be missing: those who are ostentatious in polite company are detested as much as those who air blasphemous opinions in the domain of an Established Church. But once we realize that even the pettiest error of behaviour is seen by Swift as a symptom of one huge degenerative disease, and that the little symptom puts him in mind instantly of the great evil that has occasioned it, we understand again that we are dealing with one who can think only in terms of unities. We cease to be surprised by the reckless way he broadcasts his anger or to wonder why a figure of such eminence spent twenty years sourly collecting samples of contemporary small-talk, cant and jargon. For if conversation and language reached their perfection in the reign of Charles I, every decline from this lingual perfection must serve as a reminder that all else in life has declined alongside it.

It is highly probable that this conviction began at a very early age and that the conception of dignity as something exemplified by the reign of the martyred king was a boyhood ideal and a very ardent one. But there are two ways in which a young man who has chosen "wit" as his instrument may use it in the service of an old ideal. The first, and most usual way, particularly in the case of clergymen, is the simple, direct way of lauding and honouring the ideal, of praising extremely those who adhere to it still and comparing them favourably with those who have fallen away from it. The second way is that of satire, which reverses the above order and shows the ideal almost entirely by ridiculing and condemning the lapses from it. Which of the two ways a "wit" will choose is a question which his personal temperament and peculiar ability will decide: moreover, he may begin by using the first way and, later, realize that the second suits him better.

We may give a straightforward, contemporary example of this change of weapons in the service of the same ideal by mentioning Mr. Evelyn Waugh, who begins his career by hymning directly his ideal of beauty and courage and then changes his method to one of attack against the present decline from those standards. The change is purely a methodical and tactical one, for the hallowed ideal remains much the same, changing only insofar as age and experience enlarge it. Mr. Waugh can at any time he pleases revert to the method with which he began and can pay direct homage to Campion simply by exchanging satire for praise. He can even, as the years pass, attempt the extremely difficult task of mixing the two methods and combining praise and satire in a single book: we find this combination, too, in *Gulliver's Travels*.

We are highly fortunate in being able to see and study clearly the ways chosen by Swift to serve his ideal. Like Mr. Waugh, he begins by serving it directly, in the shape of "Cavalier" odes and panegyrics; he then discovers that the satirical method is suited better to his energy and cast of mind. But throughout his life Swift is able to revert whenever he pleases and appeal directly to the reader's better side: he will often choose one topic and treat it, in turn, in the two different ways; for example, *A Proposal for Improving Conversation* is a highly good-natured attempt to reprieve those who are about to be hanged, drawn and quartered in *Polite Conversation*. The sermons say very plainly and gravely what the satirical writings express with enormous ingenuity and levity. God's majestic indifference to human trivia commands not only respectful obeisance but the comical illustration that appears in the pretty squib against those who refuse to eat bacon on fast-days:

> Who can believe with common Sense
> A Bacon-slice gives God offense?
> Or, how a Herring hath a Charm
> Almighty Anger to disarm?
> Wrapt up in Majesty divine,
> Does He regard on what we dine?

Both methods of upholding the ideal were available to Swift when he was young, and both appealed to him. His example in the way of open praise was the Cavalier poet Cowley; his example in the satirical way was the Cavalier satirist Butler. If he was familiar with Cowley at the age of fifteen, he was equally familiar with Butler, whose *Hudibras* he claimed still to know by heart in old age. What his early writings show is the gradual process by which a Cowley changes into a Butler.

These early poems are also a very exact guide to the unpleasing discrepancy he saw between what he wanted his wits to achieve and what they could actually accomplish. Macaulay says that when Swift went to live with Sir William Temple at the age of twenty-one he was "An eccentric, uncouth, disagreeable young Irishman, who had narrowly escaped plucking at Dublin" but who was nonetheless "conscious of his pre-eminent ability". The first of these statements may or may not be true; the second is quite wrong. Swift craved for "pre-eminent ability" at this time but was most miserably doubtful about his power to claim it. "It is certain," he wrote to Pope in later years, "that all persons of true genius have an invincible modesty and suspicion of themselves upon their first sending their thoughts into the world . . ." and this condition of painful self-doubt at odds with high hopes is expressed exactly in a very early poem:

In vain, I tug and pull the oar;
And when I almost reach the shore,
Straight the Muse turns the helm, and I launch out again,
And yet, to feed my pride,
When'er I mourn, stops my complaining breath,
With promise of a mad reversion after death.

If, beside this, we lay the two lines, written at the same early stage, that describe in small better than any others one of the principal glories of Swift's eventual genius:

> Beat not the path which vulgar feet have trod
> But give the vigorous fancy room. . . .

we see clearly the different ways in which the frustrated wit is pulling, struggling to hymn the pious and the good while not confining the energy of a "vigorous fancy", and hoping for immortality even as the chosen method of expression is proving useless.

For the early poems are simply high-minded. They express Swift's ideals and detestations, but they provide no room for the fancy and unlimited energy that mark Swift once he has found his feet. *The Ode to Sancroft* ("a gentleman I admire at a degree more than I can express") glorifies the archbishop who retained his self-respect by refusing to swear an allegiance that he believed was not due and preferred retirement to dishonour. *The Ode to Sir William Temple* tells us of an even greater respect for one who spent his life among rogues and politicians and yet emerged as pure and dignified as when he went in. Both poems display here and there in their high-mindedness short eruptions of frustrated ferocity:

> Each line shall stab, shall blast, like daggers and like fire

but the poet's intention is still to deny himself precisely that undignified pleasure:

> Check in thy satire, angry Muse . . .
> Let not the outcasts of this outcast age
> Provoke the honour of my Muse's rage. . . .

The check is not sustained for long. The balance between holy balm and corrosive acid becomes entirely unequal in the poem *To Congreve*, badly defacing the Muse whose happiness lies "in pleasing all that's good among the great". On the lady's brow appears, boldly and divinely sanctioned

> My hate, whose lash just heaven has long decreed
> Shall on a day make sin and folly bleed. . . .

and in the next and last of these early poems, the old
Muse is kicked out for ever with a hearty boot behind
her:

> And from this hour
> I here renounce thy visionary power;
> And since thy essence on my breath depends
> Thus with a puff the whole delusion ends.

We are not sorry to see it end. It was a necessary stage,
and it is as informative to Swift's biographer as it was
to Swift. But the way is now clear not only for much
better poetry but for the prose of *A Tale of a Tub*.

*   *   *

Sir Harold Williams says that we can never understand
Swift's life properly if we do not study the three volumes
of his poetry: this advice is absolutely correct. Yet
Middleton Murry tells us that "as self-description" the
half-dozen early poems are "unique", that never again
does Swift "uncover himself so much". And this, too, is
quite true, although it may seem to contradict the first
authority. The early poems show us a young amateur
deeply and personally tangled up in his material; the
later poems show a practised professional who has learnt
to stand off at a distance and express even his strongest
feelings with impersonal cunning. For once Swift has
settled on satire as his instrument, an immense change
comes into his life; and if satire was to be the cause of
his worse disappointments in life, it was also to be the
cause of his living that particular life at all. For satire
brings a peculiar sort of dignity into the life of an
idealistic man whose dream is of a time long past. So
long as he is struggling to hymn old virtues and departed
heroes, he is a man whose life is spent in a romantic
dream which is not of the world in which he lives. The
virtues and heroes in question may be valid and honourable ones, but because they have departed utterly from
the scene of the present day they exist only as nostalgic

convictions in the mind of the writer, who, in effect, must absent himself from the present and retire into an imagined past. But once this same man seizes upon the satirical method, he becomes a man of his own day, directing his full power against the world as it actually exists. He need never say openly: "I stand here for the reign of Charles the Martyr"—and be dismissed as an old-fashioned romantic; he has only to examine carefully and castigate the nasty examples of subsequent degeneration—and be accepted as both up to date and highly efficient. Moreover, if his cunning is great, as Swift's was, he can speak with the calculated disdain of an anonymous observer and, by this art, put a dignified distance between himself and his enemies. If his ridicule is feared by the living, he will be too much of a present menace to be relegated to a place among the dead, and the respect he commands by virtue of the power at his disposal cannot fail to give him calmness and self-assurance when he mixes with the sophisticated world. The author of *The Ode to Sancroft* can command, at most, the sympathy of the good-hearted; but the author of *A Tale of a Tub* can give the world a strong shake and, for better or worse, prove himself a man to be reckoned with.

Swift understood this very well. "They may talk of the *you-know-what*" (he means *A Tale of a Tub*), he wrote in *Journal to Stella*, "but, gad, if it had not been for that, I should never have been able to get the access I have had." Nor, one may add, would he have been a suitable person to mix with the great and engage in their affairs. His ideals commanded their affection, but his satirical pen demanded that the affection be mixed with extreme respect. For the wit, we must remember, must do service for a carriage and six horses.

These points are important, too, respecting Swift's life with Sir William Temple. Swift was ten years, on and off, with Temple, and it is reasonable enough to believe that daily contact with Temple and his world gave considera-

ble polish to Swift and taught him how to deal confi-
dently and urbanely with important people.

We may also credit Temple with having taught Swift
a great deal about how to write good prose, for Swift
never lost his admiration for Temple's writing and "preferred him to all others" long after Temple's death. But
we should not, perhaps, attribute to Temple a sophisticated assurance in Swift that came to him, more probably, through his discovery of his satirical power. Even
if we accept Macaulay's guess and see a churlish Swift
shambling up the drive to Moor Park in heavy brogues,
to depart years later a polished man-of-the-world—which
is how the cinema would show it, of course—we must still
remind ourselves that if the influence of Temple supplied
the social experience and polish, *A Tale of a Tub* created
the self-confidence. For Swift is, above all, a wit, and
though introductions to the King and revelations of high
society can be extremely useful to a nervous, ambitious
beginner, they cannot hope to give him the serene
aplomb that is satire's sweetest gift to idealism.

*   *   *

What *was* Swift like as a young man? We long to see
some physical image of him—some portrait or pen-picture
of a creature that walked and talked, and laughed and
struggled. Was the abundant energy there from the
beginning, and if it was, what sort of personal appearance did it make? But it is useless to ask, because nobody
can answer: we have nothing but little hints. Swift says
that as a student, he was of a "cold temper and uncon-
fined humour" and was told once "that my mind was like
a conjured spirit, that would do mischief if I would not
give it employment". The Earl of Orrery, his first biographer, says that the young Swift suffered from a "morose-
ness of temper" which "rendered him very unacceptable
to his companions [at Trinity College]", so that he was
"little regarded and less loved". Such descriptions have

their use because we can trace from them the grim characteristics that led, with age and frustration, to the fierce,
indignant Dean we know so well.

The trouble is that we know this "character" *too* well
and are apt to think it is true and complete. Even the
earliest portrait, painted when Swift was in his thirties,
presents a very square, unyielding face, with so slight a
suggestion of cordiality in the features that the most we
could give it by way of a caption would be Orrery's
words: "He was sour and severe, but not absolutely ill-
natured." As time passes, and the young wit becomes a
dean and a patriot, the face lengthens into high austerity
and clerical propriety, while legend plays about the long
wig in the shape of swooping cherubs bearing ribbons of
grateful inscription: one would not imagine that the digni-
tary before one was turning out some of his least dignified
verses at the time. When the wig is stripped off at last,
in Orrery's frontispiece, and we see suddenly a Churchillian head shaped like a cannon-ball, and fronted by beetle
brows, bulbous eyes and a decisive but curiously pendu-
lous nose, we feel more than ever that we have looked
upon the rancorous energy and the pugnacity but been
deprived entirely of the punster who said that Alexander
the Great derived his name from a fondness for fried
eggs (All Eggs Under the Grate) and that Aristophanes
had too much "Airy Stuff in 'is" head. That a certain
front was kept up we may deduce from the fact that
Swift never laughed, preferring, contrary to the rest of
humanity, to suck in his cheeks rather than expand them
when he enjoyed a joke: this, of course, is what irony *is*.
But he seems to have been excellent company, to have
been very fond of being among women, and to have
spent at least half his time in humorous amusement—
"nor showed the parson in his gait and face". Orrery even
says that he once raced a fellow-parson to church, win-
ning by an aisle's length and horrifying the congregation;
he also says that when Swift found his church empty

save for his clerk Roger he proceeded promptly with the service, saying, "Dearly beloved ROGER, the scripture moveth you and me in sundry places . . ." and so on to the very end.

Of course, one cannot vouch for such stories, but one can vouch for the fact that the Earl was shocked repeatedly by the Dean, because the Earl says so and, like so many after him, feels that Swift's religion came much too close to ribaldry. Orrery, like most of us, found it hard to see in one person the divine who preached so authoritatively "in a strong, nervous voice" and the priest who appeared at times to be a leaf from the pages of *Gargantua and Pantagruel*. He was also as puzzled as Dr. Johnson was by Swift's extreme passion for long walks: when he went to England, he "often went in a waggon" but "more frequently walked from Holyhead to Leicester, London, or any other part. . . . He generally chose to dine with waggoners, hostlers, and persons of that rank; and he used to lie at night in houses where he found written over the door *Lodgings for a Penny*". "He delighted", Orrery goes on, "in scenes of low life. . . . The vulgar dialect was not only a fund of humour for him, but I verily believe was acceptable to his nature; otherwise I know not how to account for the many filthy ideas, and indecent expressions . . . that will be found throughout his works".

Of course, no young man who has been to a university need go to waggoners and hostlers for filthy ideas and indecent expressions; but we should not, simply for this reason, dismiss Orrery's report as romantic. There is no doubt that all through *A Tale of a Tub* we feel we are reading a man who knows something about vulgar life as it is led by those who are born to it. Covering great distances, whether afoot or on horseback, was a lifelong obsession: if the weather was too foul, the Dean would run repeatedly up and down the deanery stairs. *Lodgings for a Penny* suggests the man who was poor most of his life, loved economy and, at the height of his power with the Queen's ministers, was still in lodgings and would carefully pick the unburned coals off his bedroom fire when he went to bed, to save them for the next day. As for the "vulgar dialect", it was most certainly a fund of humour for him: what he most abominated in polite society, he most enjoyed outside it; it was always his relief from his own severity. When he satirized the powerful he loved to do so by pulling them down to the level of the vulgar, implying that this was the appropriate level for persons who had betrayed all that birth, breeding, riches and power could give them. Their swinishness, their poxes, their boozing and their gusting indicated the course that their castigation should take: if they would not uphold propriety, they would be treated with none. And though we can never hope to understand Swift, or put him neatly together under a particular heading, we can at least see that what he satirized was present in himself and that it took very little to swing him violently from culture to coarseness and from dignity to savagery. The High Churchman who ridicules the Dissenters does so with an "enthusiasm" that would shock any Presbyterian; the upholder of the "golden mean" supports, really, nothing but one of his own more amiable moods. If we refuse to accept Swift as an idealist of dignity and a man of rigid, passionate principles, we cannot hope to understand why he is driven so easily by any betrayal of these into the most scabrous rages and revengeful emotions. His wiser friends understand this very well, and refused flatly to credit the misanthropy and disdain of the human race that we, today, believe to have been true of Swift. "If you despised the world as much as you pretend, and perhaps believe", Bolingbroke tells him coolly, "you would not be so angry with it".

We are far less understanding in this matter today. We allow no distinction to be made between the person of

Swift and the art of Swift. When Gulliver's revulsion extends at last to the whole human race we reject not only the fictitious conclusion but the man who wrote it. We react to *A Tale of a Tub* in exactly the spirit of Queen Anne, denying the possibility that so much coarseness and vehemence can be expressed by a priest who is truly religious. In this way we not only deny the writer of fiction his need to push satire as far as it will go, but deny the priest his right to uphold a High Church orthodoxy in the teeth of his enemies. When certain of the saints assure us that we are a good-for-nothing pack of scoundrels and mere belly-bags of excrement, disgusting in the Lord's sight, we not only regard them as indubitably pious but point to their disgust as evidence of their piety; similarly, when Dante shows us over Hell and points out our human flesh being boiled or frozen stiff we respond with a high respect for the poet and a mournful acceptance of his message. That we should refuse to do as much for Swift is very unimaginative on our part and very unjust to him: we carry on down through the centuries precisely the disapproval that ruined him when he was alive. Although this is the greatest possible tribute to his continuing power, it is also evidence of our continuing inability to see an honest relationship between satire and religion. It is not the humour we mind, for we accept that readily enough in *The Praise of Folly* and admire Erasmus the more for it. Nor is it the bawdy, for we are prepared to come to terms with *Gargantua and Pantagruel* and see how a priest may become a sort of Friar Tuck without basic loss of piety. What we cannot accept is a mind more sophisticated than Rabelais' and more ferocious than Erasmus': it is the blending of the Church Militant with the "vigorous fancy" that distresses us. We cannot trust the orthodoxy because we distrust the overwhelming energy behind it: Murry even goes so far as to insist that "a hierarchy of values cannot be maintained in the presence of the comic spirit" and that Swift "never wrote anything more patently absurd than when, in 1709, he attempted to excuse *A Tale of a Tub* as a service done to the Church of England".

The answer to this is that though God has always had definite limitations imposed upon His behaviour by those who believe in Him, today he is particularly circumscribed and many of the duties He performed in the past are no longer considered to be consonant with His honour and glory. He has for some time now been so fixedly on the watch for the fall of the sparrow that we can no longer imagine Him in the more aquiline role that was once considered fitting to His dignity. It was the Dissenters who began the "levelling" process of divinity that seems natural today and to whose hearts and minds God dispatched confidential information about His secret wishes and dearest hopes—and it is precisely to those Dissenters and their descendants of today that Swift opposes himself, expressing horror at the idea of God's being made party to the discreditable wrangles and self-centred tumults of degenerate priests— an impropriety which he compares very nicely to the use of the *deus ex machina* in cheap theatricals:

For, I think, it is in life as in tragedy, where it is held a conviction of great defect, both in order and invention, to interpose the assistance of praeturnatural power, without an absolute and last necessity. . . . Who that sees a little paltry mortal, droning, and dreaming, and drivelling to a multitude, can think it agreeable to common good sense, that either Heaven or Hell should be put to the trouble of influence or inspection, upon what he is about?

❄　　　❄　　　❄

This last quotation has much to tell us about Swift's attitude to human behaviour. His God cannot be said to be "in our hearts and in our understanding"; on the contrary, the immensity of His mercy is shown by the patience He displays towards hearts and understandings that ignore His existence or fly it as the pennant of their egoism. Moreover, in nothing has God shown greater mercy than in having deigned not only to sketch out the necessary rules of human conduct but even to promise salvation to those who are prepared to obey them. In a sense, therefore, God's work has already been done, and done with the utmost magnanimity: to involve Him in the shabby and contemptible irreverences that constitute most human behaviour is the degraded, theatrical trick of "dramatists" who are too stupid or too depraved to work according to His rules: they invoke God precisely because they refuse to be responsible for their own acts. And on the rare occasions when they recognize their corruptions of the rules and admit to their transgressions, they are no less irresponsible, in that they then bring on stage an *infernal* machine and produce the Devil from it as smartly as before they produced God:

> The Devil ready stands, my Swift,
> To help our fancy at a Lift . . .
> So when poor *Irish rapparee*,
> Is sentenc'd to the fatal *Tree*,
> Or naughty Boy elopes from School,
> Or pretty Miss has play'd the Fool,
> And crack'd her tender *Maidenhead*
> With lying on too hard a Bed,
> Their loads they all on *Satan* lay:
> The Devil did the Deed, not they!
>
> —*A Panegyric on Dean Swift*

And yet, as Swift is never tired of declaring, the divine rules are of the simplest and plainest sort: they demand obedience, but no particular intelligence and certainly no art. Indeed, the evidence, Swift suggests, shows clearly that God has taken care not to make his rules too difficult for the Lilliputians whom He has condescended to guide. The laws of good government, for example, are of the simplest kind: government, Swift insists, demands nothing in the way of brains and acuteness and has been

so nicely adjusted by Providence to the capacities of
ordinary persons that it suffers, rather than benefits, when
talented men bring their ingenuity to bear upon its simplicity. If "Politicks are nothing but Corruptions", this is
only because the politician's beginnings and ends are
calculated rejections of the laws of God and are based
upon arts of cunning inspired solely by human ambition
and vanity. Swift says, we deem it *necessary* to befoul
the simplicity of things in order to show that we are
extraordinary: goodness disappoints our love of ostentation. ("Harry Killigrew said to Lord Wharton, 'You
would not swear at this Rate, if you thought you were
doing GOD Honour!'") An excellent example of the way
it continues to disappoint us is the attitude we take
towards Martin, the representative of approximate goodness in *A Tale of a Tub*. Save for his goodness, Martin
is, as Murry complains, "a nonentity". He keeps his
father's coat in the best possible shape. Instead of rant-
ing with Jack and vaunting it with Peter, he has little
to say: "he is simply a negation—not Jack and not Peter".
We may complain, justly, that such a character is a
theatrical disappointment, but perhaps we should admit
also that we find him a *human* disappointment as well.
For we have no desire to resemble Martin. Goodness has
not the exciting qualities of evil; we depend on the latter
to make life interesting. That, as Swift saw, is the principal reason why it is usually so beastly.

If a man begins with the assumption that goodness is
boring—which it usually is—there is no limit to which
he will not go in order to avoid it. All Swift's satire is
directed against the hundreds of ways that human beings
have discovered of avoiding being good; all his benevolence goes to those who have resisted the ostentation of
being bad—who would rather be a mere negation of evil
than a distinguished example of it. When we protest
against such a point of view, scorning it as passive and
uninteresting, we not only show our disdain for good-

ness, but make ourselves, without knowing it, the essential object of satire. To appreciate thoroughly what Swift
is doing, we must never read him without appreciating
fully our settled determination to make our lives supply
him with the material from which his books are made.

It may be thought that Swift shows intolerance in this
matter and has no proper right to denounce badness so
haughtily. So one must stress the fact that he is, on the
contrary, as magnanimous as is the God in which he
believes. Swift is not a Pelagian; he would be disgusted
by the very idea that human beings might achieve the
perfection of Christ. He asks no more than a bare recognition of the moral superiority of goodness and a strong
effort to pursue it: this, surely, is not asking too much.
The more he mixes with the world, the less good he
expects it to be and the less goodness he asks of its
inhabitants: the spirit of the *Ode to Sancroft* is soon
dropped, because it demands far too much. Swift does
not expect any Christian actually to *be* a Christian; he
only suggests that they should keep a Christian aim in
mind and practise a minimal amount of it. If they find
this too much, he is prepared to compromise and suggest
that they try merely to go through the motions of Christianity: if they do this regularly, he thinks, they may one
day understand what it is they are doing, and what
began as clockwork may end by being heart-felt. Even
kings, Swift says, can be a great help in this matter,
because by choosing as ministers men who go through
the motions of Christianity, they can convince the ambitious that Christianity is no stumbling-block in the way
of greatness. Moreover, once this form of preferment has
become customary and the king finds himself forever
surrounded by Christian ministers, there is a chance
that even he himself may become a Christian too.
Should this happen, the teachings of Christ might move
mountains; for Christianity could not fail to become all
the rage if the figure of Christ were upheld not merely

by the Head of the Church but by the Prince of Courtiers.
An idle dream, this, however; for Swift knows that if it
is difficult for the ordinary subject to become more than
a nominal Christian, the difficulties in the way of the
King must be insuperable. We cannot ask a man who
has lived all his life from the cradle onwards in an atmos-
phere of total corruption to reach the decent status of a
grocer.

It is at this point that we should begin to obtain relish
and delight from Swift's satire, for we are here at the
very centre of its ingenious web. We know before we
read him that he is in the true line of high satire—that
like Aristophanes and Juvenal his aim is to reform the
"knights" and "emperors" of the world and improve
society from the top: this means, of course, that the
"highest" must struggle to *rise* to the level of the "lowest". We regard him very properly as a High Church
Tory and as one who upholds the existing order of his
world, but we appreciate very little the price that Swift
demands of the mighty for his advocacy on their behalf.
For Swift says, like a hundred other High Churchmen,
that each man must be content with his lot and that all
must swear allegiance to their rightful king; but his
reasons for demanding this orthodox stability and the
arguments he presents for loyalty and quiesence show
such horrible contempt for lords and princes that these
great men, were they clever enough to understand what
Swift was doing, would find any social rebel of a radical
persuasion infinitely less menacing than so terrible a
Tory. The king must be supported—but why? Because he
is too contemptible a creature to support himself: his
condition is so degraded and pitiful, his mind and body
so warped and ailing, that no good-hearted subject can
see his predicament without wishing to extend to him a
loyalty that springs as much from mercy as from a wish
for social stability. The peers about the king must never
be envied or resented by the long-suffering poor—but

why? Again, because their lot is so miserable and contemptible: they are men doomed to go through life without knowledge of the common decencies and afflicted
even unto death with the sourest miseries that selfishness
and wanton stupidity can provide. Here is Swift pro-
claiming these things from the very pulpit in language
of quite majestic perfection:

. . . I shall therefore show, first, that the Poor . . . do enjoy
many temporal Blessings, which are not common to the Rich
and Great; and likewise, that the Rich and Great are subject
to many temporal Evils, which are not common to the
Poor. . . .

As to the first: Health, we know, is generally allowed to
be the best of all earthly Possessions. . . . For Riches are
of no Use, if Sickness taketh from us the ability of enjoying
them. . . . Now, if we would look for Health, it must be in
the humble Habitation of the labouring Man, or industrious
Artificer, who earn their Bread by the Sweat of their
Brows. . . .

The Refreshment of the Body by Sleep is another great
Happiness of the meaner Sort. Their Rest is not disturbed by
the Fear of Thieves and Robbers, nor is it interrupted by
Surfeits of Intemperance. . . . As to Children, which are certainly accounted of as a Blessing, even to the Poor . . . they
are an Assistance to their honest Parents, instead of being a
Burthen; they are healthy and strong, and fit for Labour;
neither is the Father in Fear, lest his Heir should be ruined
by an unequal Match. . . .

The poorer Sort are not the objects of General Hatred. . . .
[They] are safest in Times of publick Disturbance, in perilous
Seasons, and publick Revolutions. . . . But in such Seasons,
the Rich are the publick Mark, because they are oftentimes
of no Use, but to be plundered; like some Sort of Birds, who
are good for nothing but their Feathers. . . .

Let us proceed on the other Side to examine the disadvan-
tages that the Rich and Great lye under. . . .

First then; While Health, as we have said, is the general Portion of the lower Sort, the Gout, the Dropsy, the Stone, the Cholick, and all other Diseases are continually haunting the Palaces of the Rich and Great, as the natural Attendants upon Laziness and Luxury. . . .

Business, Fear, Guilt, Design, Anguish, and Vexation are continually buzzing about the Curtains of the Rich and Powerful, and will hardly suffer them to close their Eyes, unless they are dozed with the Fumes of strong Liquors. . . .

If Riches were so great a Blessing as they are commonly thought, they would at least have this Advantage, to give their Owners chearful Hearts and Countenances; they would often stir them up to express their Thankfulness to God. . . . But, in Fact, the contrary to all this is true. For where are there more cloudy Brows, more melancholy Hearts, or more Ingratitude to their great Benefactor, than among those who abound in Wealth. . . ?

I know not one real advantage that the Rich have over the Poor, except the Power of doing good to others: But this is an Advantage which God hath not given wicked Men the grace to make use of. The Wealth acquired by evil Means was never employed to good Ends; for that would be to divide the Kingdom of Satan against itself. Whatever hath been gained by Fraud, Avarice, Oppression, and the like, must be preserved and increased by the same Methods.

I shall add but one Thing more upon this Head. . . . God (whose Thoughts are not as our Thoughts) never intended Riches or Power to be necessary for the Happiness of Mankind in this life; because it is certain, that there is not one single good Quality of the Mind absolutely necessary to obtain them . . . neither Honour, Justice, Temperance, Wisdom, Religion, Truth or Learning. . . .

This excellent and delightful sermon clarifies many of the perplexities we have about Swift. First, it shows that though the clergyman who preached it was an *unusual* clergyman, he was not a *false* one. He recognized, that is to say, two sorts of existence—that of human beings, thinking chiefly in terms of human ambition, and that of their Maker, "whose Thoughts are not our Thoughts". Secondly, he found the widest gap between the human and the divine to be represented by those who had climbed highest in the human scale, and he demanded of the poor a generous pity and respect for the misfortunes of their betters. Only when we understand this thoroughly can we understand why so high a Tory as Swift could be such a popular patriot and how he could combine in his own person a profound respect for authority in theory and an absolute disgust for authority in practice. We may, if we please, insist upon seeing him as a spokesman for a "closed society", but we must consider, too, the outrageous opinions he embodied in this demand. If we put ourselves in the rich man's pew and imagine ourselves listening to this sermon of Swift's, we see at once that though we might not go sorrowing away from it, we should not feel that the preacher had conferred either dignity or stability upon our station. ". . . of no Use, but to be plundered; like some Sort of Birds, who are good for nothing but their Feathers"—could any peacock hear this without *goose flesh?*

*   *   *

The student of Swift could, if he pleased, describe all Swift's opinions in terms of *nakedness* and *clothing*. Naked we come into the world, naked we go out of it: in between that beginning and that end, we cover ourselves. The Lord gives us a bare skin; what we hang on it is of human art and must not be attributed to our Maker. Because we are more sophisticated about covering ourselves than our aboriginal fathers were, we must expect our efforts to show some absurd signs of human artifice: these we must not only keep to a minimum but keep to a minimum which is not too noticeable. For if vanity and ambition are evident in ostentatious plumage, they are equally evident in the flaunting of shabby rags—

what the coxcomb achieves by means of one extreme, the canting Dissenter achieves by its opposite. This is one of the prettiest touches in *A Tale of a Tub*: the mob fails to distinguish between Peter's gaudy plumage and Jack's lurid tatters. Swift took this little story from an anecdote about Diogenes the Stoic (who *lived* in a tub!), and it pleased him not only because it suited his ideas but because the whole business of clothing fascinated him all his life. As Dean of St. Patrick's he was a friend and adviser to all sorts of artificers in Dublin, but it was the weavers he loved best and helped most; and it was as a "Drapier" that he chose to speak to "the Whole People of Ireland". We are never far from cloth, scissors and thread in *Gulliver's Travels*—little tailors and their assistants climb over the huge body of the Man-mountain in Lilliput and contrive to take his measure and stitch him a suit; in Brobdignag, the silks of that country hang like ponderous woolens upon the little mannikin, though they make, for giants, "a very grave and decent habit". The intellectuals of Laputa express their metaphysics through the absurdity of their garments: in the world of the Houyhnhnms, rabbit skins and the pelt of the *nnuhnoh* make adequate suits and stockings, while for the stout soles of shoes there are "the skins of *Yahoos* dried in the sun".

Clothing is necessary to man. It is not only necessary for warmth and comfort, it is necessary as an aid to civilized behaviour. The human body is a gross thing; it exudes the physical beast in man just as "Liberty of Conscience" exudes his beastliness of heart. When Christianity is absent, the appearance of it must be put on; and so long as the body provides evidence of the animal, it, too, must be given a fair cover. This fact is acknowledged not only by the prudish Swift but by the ladies and gentlemen of his society who spend most of their lives pretending, through artifice, to be other than what they are. We may scorn such an attitude today, but we share it nonetheless: very few of us obtain much pleasure from sweat and excrement, and though from time to time we make valuable sorties back into "Nature", the bath always wins in the end: by now, in fact, it has rendered nakedness tolerable and even pleasing. But in eras of rotten teeth, dirty skins and smelly close-stools, our naked selves lacked many of the attractions they present today, and the disparity between man naked and man clothed provides endless satisfaction to the satirist. Nor does he need to reflect very long upon this disparity without seeing that it is simply one example of an over-all disparity—of the great general gap that separates man plain and man ornamented. The wise and civilized man is at pains always to mend this gap as unobtrusively as possible; he keeps his body in good repair by living soberly, and he chooses for its covering a habit of like sobriety. The unlettered countryman often achieves much the same simple end by living in ignorance of fashion and by lacking the money to defeat his simplicity. But once a man has got a little foothold in a more sophisticated and voguish world, all manner of clothing becomes necessary to his vanity. Neither his body nor his soul is safe from the artifices he employs on it: the gap, to him, is not between animal nakedness and human decency, but between what is commonplace and what is admired. A vast, world-wide charade smothers all human simplicity and dignity and leaves nothing unaffected by its vanity and ostentation. This is the world that Swift sees and by which he is obsessed—and this is the world to which he retorts by reminding it with incessant ferocity and in the foulest language of the exudations and stinks that lie below the silks and plumage. The ostentatious artifice becomes a glaring denial of the truth, the existence of which is no longer recognized by the lady who has spent five hours obliterating it:

She knows her Early Self no more,
But fill'd with Admiration, stands, '
As Other Painters oft adore
The Workmanship of their own Hands. . . .
　　　　　　　—The Progress of Beauty

The beau, who sees this vision passing in her carriage, accepts it as the real self—as well he may. For he has hidden his own pox under gaudy breeches and can deny, with ruffles, wig and silk cravat, the decayed animal within. Yet there must always come that awful night when both charlatans, stripped suddenly of their respective duplicities, must appear to one another in all their natural rottenness and physical debasement.

Swift has described this moment of disillusion so often and so grossly that in the end he makes us think *more* kindly of the masquerading wretches—just as we think *more* kindly of the Dissenter, once Swift has knelt upon him: the satirical punishment is far more terrible than its recipient. But we get more sense of proportion, more understanding of his ferocity, if we take our eyes off its particular victims and realize that a general condition is being attacked. False plumage and its ostentatious lies appear more strikingly in the form of clothes, paint and ornaments, but these pretences are only superficial evidences of much deeper corruptions. The beau who falsifies the naked truth of his body is the divine who corrupts the Gospels with his fashionable glosses. He is the courtier who prefers the polished lie to the plain statement, the fop who hides his mental defectiveness in a voguish vocabulary. He is the bishop whose lawn sleeves have been bought out of the stipends of poor curates, the king who prefers flattery to honesty. He is the politician who has learnt how to disguise greed as a service to the nation and put a show of efficiency upon dishonesty. The painted belle with the dirty body is not only disgusting in herself; she is also the vehicle that passes down the generations all the pretences, vanities and vapid aims that make social degeneration a fixed condition. If she excites Swift's particular horror it is because she must feign so much if she is to be a lady instead of a woman; modesty must be discarded in favour of prudery; the vixen of bedroom intrigue must be shocked by any suggestion of coarseness and pretend to as much terror in the presence of a man as she would at the sight of a mouse. And these hypocrisies must reach an extreme of disgustingness when she makes her pious devotions to religion:

> In Church, secure behind her Fan
> She durst behold that Monster, Man. . . .
> Or on that Matt devoutly kneeling
> Would lift her Eyes up to the Ceeling,
> And heave her Bosom unaware
> For neighb'ring Beaux to see it bare.

Swift deals with this as many still deal with a puppy— as it scampers prettily from the living-room, he seizes it, drags it back onto the carpet and rubs its nose in that which it has bequeathed to posterity. His insistence on doing this, and the satisfaction he gets from it, have worried all his admirers from Orrery to Murry: it has even been suggested that towards the end of his life, Swift was obsessed by an "excremental vision". This conclusion is too romantic. Obscenity is always one of Swift's retorts to degeneracy, and he makes it more frequently as he grows older and more desperate. But he has many other ways of retorting: his satire is very extensive and his medicines are never monotonous. It is we ourselves who fix so much attention on its excremental expressions, in part because they shock us but also because we tend to believe nowadays that in studying an author's character we should look to the excrement if we are to find the fundament. It would be absurd to deny that Swift pelted prudes with turds, but no four-letter word obsessed him more than *Scot*.

❊   ❊   ❊

The nature of Swift's God has more to tell us about his character than his indecencies have. If, to him, there is always a horrible gap between the honest man and the degenerate man, there is a far greater one between even the best of men and the Creator, added to which there is little in the way of an intermediating Christ. As we have seen, Swift refuses to involve either God or the Devil in the affairs of the human race; both have stated their case and done their work; the rest is up to human beings themselves. Not only is Swift's God quite out of bounds of human cognizance, He is also virtually put on the shelf. He may not be discussed, His nature may not be speculated upon; He is a closed book that exists, practically speaking, only in the few chapters of rules and revelations that He has vouchsafed to man.

Such a God is a perfectly defensible God, and it is easy to see that one might wish to stress His remoteness in a period when evangelical enthusiasm is making for too much intimacy. But just as Swift's satire is often too tremendous for the petty vices it satirizes, so is his God almost disproportionately great for the little creatures He has made. They are allowed no connection with Him at all; they are scarcely urged to pray to Him for strength. Only His laws exist, as it were, and almost the whole duty of His priest is to keep the chickens' noses to the chalked lines.

Two points concerning this "Mosaic" God deserve special attention. The first is that because He presides only in the form of His plain laws, no metaphysics and only the minimum of theology can be allowed in regard to Him. Religious speculation is not merely a mistake but an evil, in that it diverts the mind from practical obedience into meaningless abstractions. For the same reason, all philosophy must be of a severely practical sort: a man may ask *"Quid est imperium?"*—"What is government?"—but once he asks "What is contained in the idea of government?" he embarks on a sort of enquiry that is pernicious because it is essentially fantastic. Swift traced the beginnings of the iniquitous habit to John Locke and was able, in consequence, to class it with all other degenerations that had occurred since the time of Charles I. But we, taking a broader view, may see it as a much older quarrel—the old quarrel between satirist and philosopher that is found in *The Clouds*. To the philosopher, the satirist is not a thinker at all; to the satirist, the philosopher is one who has no serious interest in religion and morality. Swift's intelligence was unsuited in every way to philosophical considerations—and the God in whom he believed was exactly like himself, a very plain-speaking person to whom theologians were entirely abhorrent.

This is illustrated very exactly by the second point respecting Swift's God—His view of charity. For most of us, now, charity is a wide conception of general outlook: as "caritas" or "compassion" it describes an attitude to life, a necessary emotion, rather than a law of practical behaviour. The State supplies assistance to those who are in need; the charity supplied by us is mainly sympathetic, forgiving and affectionate. But where we are broad, emotional and vague, Swift was limited and strictly practical. He saw charity almost entirely in terms of money, and in obedience to God's demands he practised charity generously in his lifetime and left all his money to charity after his death. Yet his life was not an example of what we call charitable impulses. It was severe, dogmatic, unimpartial and unforgiving. We, who compassion all mankind more readily than we give cheques to individual persons, are puzzled by a man who found it hard to forgive but was ready to fork out. Ours, we feel, is the religious attitude; the Dean's charity is simply philanthropy.

Clearly, there are weaknesses on both sides in these different views of charity. Our own view is a perfect target for satire, for we become most certainly satirical objects when we spend our compassion limitlessly but keep a firm hold on our cash: we might almost be accused of spending the one in order to keep the other. But once we have admitted this we are free to say that the reverse is also true and that the spirit of charity is not fulfilled if we spend money in order to save our emotions. It would be unjust to say that this was what Swift did, but when we consider both the remoteness of his God and the strictly practical nature of his charity we do suspect that both attitudes were those of a man who found emotional expenditure extremely painful and preferred to withhold it in his relations to both God and man. This was not because he was a cold man, but because when his feelings were strongly affected—as they often were—his will-power and self-command disappeared and he was plunged into the chaos of unmanageable emotion. That is why he hews so strictly to the Law and does his utmost to impose on himself and others an order and discipline that will prevent emotional anarchy.

This stringency may seem regrettable in his personal life, particularly in regard to his relations with women; yet it is the quality that makes him our greatest satirist. For it is not Swift's native energy and capacious indignation that gives power to his prose: this power comes from the tightness with which it is ordered—the way in which the most violent feeling is subjected and constricted, so that instead of welling out in an aimless flood, like a fact of nature or a furious letter to a newspaper, it is made to work like a fireman's hose, obtaining velocity and accuracy from that which confines it: this, surely, is the meaning of Goethe's famous dictum *"In der Beschränkungen zeigt sich erst der Meister"*. When the emotion behind the art is merely amused or contemptuous the strictures that are laid upon it are proportionately light and easy, as in the *Bickerstaff Papers* or the amiable irony of *An Argument against Abolishing Christianity*: he smiled as he wrote; we smile as we read. But when

the emotions begin to boil, every effort is made to tie
them into the narrowest possible form of expression: the
more sanguinary the blood, the more refined the vein.
The horror of *A Modest Proposal* is *in* the modesty with
which the proposal is uttered: the tone of it is most
beautifully tentative: we are dealing, it appears, with a
good man who thinks it would be a good thing to eat
babies but will drop the idea immediately if anyone can
think of one or two sensible reasons why it should not be
done.

The same horror, tied with metrical exactitude and
silky soliloquy, is shown by the great poem *On Dreams*,
wherein Swift reflects that what we do by day we dream
by night:

> For, when in Bed we rest our weary limbs,
> The Mind unburthen'd sports in various whims,
> The Busy Head with mimick Art runs o'er
> The Scenes and Actions of the Day before. . .

> The Soldier smiling hears the Widows Cries
> And stabs the Son before the Mother's Eyes.
> With like Remorse his Brother of the Trade,
> The Butcher, feels the Lamb beneath his blade. . .

> The kind Physician grants the Husband's Prayers,
> Or gives Relief to long-expecting Heirs.
> The sleeping Hangman ties the fatal Noose,
> Nor unsuccessful waits for dead Men's Shoes. . . .

When Swift loses this constrictive control, or refuses
deliberately to make use of it, his power disappears at
once. Letters between friends, for instance, he believed
should be written artlessly and he tried not to "lean upon
my Elbow" when writing them. Consequently, his letters
are always a pleasure but rarely an expression of formida-
ble energy. The same dissipation marks those poems in
which the restraint was not adequate to the pressure; and
it is very marked, of course, in the frenzied outbursts and
revulsions of his personal life. For when Swift loses control his feelings become unmanageable and he loses

everything that is most dear to him; dignity, stability, charity and common sense are swept away by rage, revenge, suspicion and spite. He becomes at once the easy target of cooler heads and can be made to look very silly by those who have the courage to answer him back or the magnanimity to refuse to quarrel with him.

To look silly is certainly the last thing Swift wants. His position, his independence, his dignity, all depend on his authority's being accepted and respected by others. This will not be the case if *either* party to the arrangement is a slave to passion and turbulent emotion. Hence the necessity of inflexible rules of behaviour, which the Dean struggles to impose not only on himself but on the whole society in which he lives. Hence, too, a God who is above all a law-maker—a God of discipline whose other attributes should be of no concern to human beings.

This God is a familiar figure in England; so is his prophet. Both belong more to the educational field than to the religious one, which is what gives them a more earthly than heavenly quality. Our Dean's religion need never be doubted, but it may be seen as the sort of religion that inspires great headmasters. These awe-inspiring teachers may derive their authority from God, but they give their whole attention to the behaviour of their pupils. Their interest is not in speculating upon the Lawgiver but in obtaining human obedience to His rules. Salvation is not within the headmaster's province, but instruction is, and so is discipline. Most headmasters have only a school of children, but all England was Swift's school, and all his children were grown people. In actual children he was usually uninterested: his teaching was only for those that were old enough to benefit from it. True children he bore with as an inevitable nuisance.

We have no difficulty in understanding *furious* headmasters. They are out of fashion now, but until recently they were an essential part of education. We find nothing odd or mysterious in the fact that when they were obeyed they were urbane, dignified, impressive and agreeable but that disobedience turned them into punitive fiends. The man to whom authority is of the first importance is the man most tempted to behave outrageously when his authority is rejected. His violence does not recognize normal bounds because his sense of authority, too, is of an abnormal sort. The pupil who calls him a "just beast" makes the phrase memorable because it unites so aptly words that would stand normally in strict opposition to one another.

Can we doubt that Swift was such a man? In what other sort of person can we unite moral authority and abnormal violence? All Swift's relations with women, for example, bespeak a man of this kind—an unyielding educator with inflexible standards. Hester Johnson was only his first pupil—and the only one whom he caught young enough to mould completely into his system. Yet even she was watched until the day of her death by her Cerberus of a teacher, and could be charged, gently but still sternly, with showing signs of wilfulness and rebellion in middle age. When she was gone at last and Swift sat down to write her little history, it was a teacher's pain that he expressed as well as a bosom friend's—"one in whose education I may claim to have played some small part", he wrote.

Hester Johnson was his first pupil; Laetitia Pilkington was one of the Dublin school of his last years and was taught with proportionate ferocity: the Dean pinched her arms until they were black and blue. Between Miss Johnson and Mrs. Pilkington came a whole string of young women, all of whom must turn their backs on gossip, chatter, paint and finery and take to a regime of classical studies, sober dress, outdoor exercise and sensible diet. They must learn to obey and serve their husbands, to guide their children firmly in the path of true obedience and to learn young that their charm and beauty will all be gone in a few years and will need to be replaced with attributes of intelligence and thoughtfulness. Those that responded well to this curriculum were privileged to enjoy the genius of their teacher at its gayest and most ardent; those that would not conform to its absolute demands were either thrown scornfully back into the world of paint and finery or made to squirm under black glares and hideous rages. Of all these pupils Esther Vanhomrigh seems to have understood best the nature of her tutor's vocation:

> That innocent Delight he took
> To see the Virgin mind her Book,
> Was but the Master's secret Joy
> In School to hear the finest Boy.

We know that Swift's form of love—an impassioned education—was not in tune with normal behaviour, so we suppose that the virgins and mothers who sat in his class did so reluctantly or disdainfully. This was not the case at all. To be taught by Swift, however awfully, was an accolade for any lady—and well Swift knew it. When Orrery, shocked (Orrery was *always* shocked) by the Dean's writing a most insolent poem about his pupil Lady Acheson, protested that such a portrait of "Daphne" disgraced the lady, the Dean only "burst into a fit of laughter. 'You fancy', says he, 'that you are very polite, but you are much mistaken. That lady had rather be a DAPHNE drawn by me, than a SACHARISSA by any other pencil' ".

This we can well believe. What women got from Swift was *attention*. That it was a fearless and often rough attention was probably one of its chief attractions. Women mattered to Swift—and mattered to him much more deeply than they do to the men who marry them. No woman will ever turn her back on a man who is determined to reform and reconstitute her whole nature, educate her mind, set her on the right path and make her a walking example to her own sex. She may weary, as Lady Acheson did at last, of having to go for long walks through brambles, read Bacon's essays interminably, hear herself rebuked regularly for inattention, disobedience and fondness for light company, as well as submit to be mocked as "snipe", "skinny" and "slattern". But all this means real attention. It even means that the woman *commands* attention—and no woman ever objected to doing that. But it is also, unfortunately, a sort of attention that wives give to husbands more often than they receive it from them. Men like Swift are never husbands. They are priests, they are teachers, they are celibates, they are homosexuals. If they do encourage maidens to marry, it is only because marriage is customary and convenient to women, and because, as Swift says drily, "time takes off from the lustre of virgins in all other eyes but mine."

The problem that arises from such attention is one of natural appetite for more. The old story of Pygmalion and Galatea tells us that when the teacher has moulded the desired image he cannot resist falling in love with his handiwork; but the new story of this kind of relationship, as told by Shaw, reverses this outcome: the inspired image falls in love with the creator. This, the Irish version, was the one that Swift experienced. His supposed marriage to his most successful creation, Hester Johnson, is in itself of interest only to the gossip columnist: in this respect it is as trifling as the question of his legitimate birth. But it does matter insofar as it tells us that after thirty years of learning to be the perfect pupil Miss Johnson was still—a woman. She knew the rules by heart, she knew what must never be asked of the master who had made them. By asking nonetheless—if ask she did— she showed that even the best-behaved pupil cannot resist the attention that has made her what she is. The day must come when the teacher of women finds—to his rage and horror—that the *principal* lesson has never been

learnt at all. That is the lesson that says that the distance
between teacher and pupil must always be maintained,
for if that distance had not been promised, the master
would never have embarked upon the work.

What we must commend, in the end, is the fact that
Swift never married at all—never, at least, in the true
sense of the word. We know that when he was a young
clergyman he *was* prepared to marry: his proposal to
Jane Waring is clear to read, as is his assurance in the
same letter that if she will not marry him he will never
marry any other woman. But what *any* marriage of
Swift's would have been like is dreadful to imagine.
Orrery thought that he would have had a more amiable
view of children if he had become a father; we may
guess with equal propriety that being a father would
have made him worse. What Swift asked of a wife does
not exist in human nature, and the effort he would have
made to make a wife other than what she was is too
horrible to think about. When men of Swift's stamp
refuse to marry they know very well what they are doing.
They know that no woman could fail to disturb the
orderliness of their ways and their preference for solitude.
They know that their gifts do not extend to those demanded by marriage and that they can best use those
gifts outside it. Above all, they know in the matter of
sexual relations that they are not heated with the needs
and desires that are in other men: the fact that we live
in an age when sexual coolness is a cause for alarm cannot alter the fact that it was not so regarded, particularly
in clergymen, in the centuries before our own. Far from
insisting that bachelors are abnormal, we should encourage them always to come forward and declare themselves. For there is nothing in celibacy to be ashamed of;
but there is always a great deal to be ashamed of in
sexual activities that have been inspired by reading fashionable books and in marriages that have been entered
into simply so as to supply the husband with credentials.

PART TWO

THE ATTEMPT, so far, has been to give Swift's idea of himself—a picture of the principles and ambitions he claimed as his own. It is time, now, to see this idea in practice—to see the collection of personal notions embodied in a man who moves and acts in the company of others. Only in this way can we test the ideas and convictions: where they are in harmony with the actions, we may see them speaking for themselves, as it were; where they conflict with the actions, we may see the deeds as the doer's self-corrections: these are always more interesting and more accurate than correctives supplied by the biographer. No man is ever the sum of his ideals and ambitions: these are only the conditions he lays down to the world; we see the whole man only when we see how he responds to the world's retort to his conditions—how much he upholds, how much he concedes, and in what spirit he drives his bargains.

We are unable to test Swift in this way before he has reached middle age. His childhood and youth are too sparsely documented: in a total of six great volumes of letters to and from Swift, only half one volume concerns the first forty-three years of his life. The plain reason for this is that until he reached that age he was not important enough to deserve record—which is why a career that proceeded to a large extent in the usual steadyish climb from nothing to something gives instead the impression of relative ordinariness abruptly jumping into extraordinary prominence. We hear little stories on the way up and we see little sketches; but we find very little to prepare us for the fact that Swift's arrival in London, in 1710, to plead a second time the Queen's Bounty for the Church of Ireland, was thought to be a noticeable event by the politicians of the day. We know that his service with Sir William Temple prepared him for politics and gave him his *entrée* to Court. We know that as chaplain to the Earl of Berkeley, he became a familiar of London society. We know that his early pamphlet *A Discourse of the Contests and Dissensions between the Nobles and Commons in Athens and Rome (1701)* served to introduce him to the Whig leader Lord Somers and that this patron of the arts was awarded the dedication of *A Tale of a Tub*. Finally, we know that Swift's talents were highly regarded already; that though, as Orrery says, "The wits and poets of that era, were numerous and eminent", yet "shining above the rest, appeared Dr. Swift". But still we are not prepared for a rise to political eminence that no other author in English history excepting Addison has surpassed—not Marvell, not Chaucer, not Milton himself. And Swift, at first, shares our surprise, saying plainly in the *Journal to Stella*: "I did not expect to find such friends as I have done". He lists, too, the numerous people who would *like* to be his friends, declaring in the opening lines of his very first letter that "The Whigs are ravished to see me, and would lay hold on me as a twig while they are drowning, and the great men making me their clumsy apologies" (that is, for not having satisfied him on his previous visit). He continues: "Every body asks me, how I came to be so long in Ireland, as naturally as if here were my Being", and there follows an impressive list of polite courtiers—"Sir John Holland, comptroller of the household, has sent to desire my aquaintance . . ."; "Here is Mr. Brydges

the paymaster-general desiring my aquaintance . . .";
". . . a servant of Lord Halifax, to desire I would go
and dine with him . . ." We cannot dismiss these advances
as mere political flattery of a minor figure, because
within a short time we find Swift exercising power in a
real way—that is to say, as a man of such influence that
he is asked by all and sundry to put in a word for them
or plead their retention in their existing offices. Moreover, the doors did not open to Swift by magic, nor even,
as he imagined, by his own exertions. Coldly received
by the Whig leaders, Somers and Godolphin, he made
artful arrangements to get the ear of Harley, the Tory
leader. But Harley and his secretary, Erasmus Lewis,
took care to arrange that these arrangements worked.
The door that Swift imagined he was prying open was
in fact being opened from behind: the politicians' need
for him was far greater than his need for them.

If the warmth of this welcome surprised Swift, it
surprises us much more, for we cannot imagine any contemporary prime minister having the least wish to entice
a satirist into his cabinet: he would, on the contrary, try
by all means to keep one out. But Harley needed the sort
of man that is not needed by a prime minister in these
days of respectable party journalism—a writer who could
present his case to the educated members of the public.
He engaged Swift for that work alone, ignorant of his
man and expecting to reward him with presents of
money and, no doubt, preferment. He was not aware of
the Queen's prejudice against Swift and took for granted
that his political spokesman would also be presented to
the Queen and preach useful sermons to her on Sundays.
In all these matters he was wrong—but wrongest of all
in not knowing that the man he invited into his politics
would never consent to be its mouthpiece if he were not
allowed to be its schoolmaster too. Within a few months
Harley and his friends had accepted this unexpected
condition: it is to their credit that they were able to do

so. But more to our point here is that we see, for the first
time, our hero's principles and ambitions put to the test
and not wavering at all. The "surprise" element in Swift's
sudden elevation is, in truth, the strength of his own
character.

We see this character and its actions in such close
detail during the next few years that we feel no regret
at having had to wait until Swift was forty-three before
we could do so. Moreover, in the course of seeing Swift
close to, before age and exile have laid their exaggerations
upon his face, we can follow the day-to-day excitements
of an important period of history with clarity and understanding. The material at our disposal is rich, various
and delicious. The exchange of letters with Archbishop
King in Dublin introduces us to the strictly official side
of Swift's character and tells us exactly how that character was regarded by his superiors in Ireland. His
pamphlets display his politics, and his letters to his
friends his amiable, helpful qualities. Finally, that extraordinary source book, the *Journal to Stella*, combines
an unsurpassed study of daily life in Lor.don with the
most intimate portrait of Swift himself. To read all these
documents concurrently is to see one man's self from
every possible position and to watch his every faculty and
emotion in action and in response.

The first thing we note is the reappearance, in a political setting, of the mingled wariness and determination
that had marked Swift as a young poet. The *Journal* tells
us (perhaps it is Swift telling himself) that Swift's mission is only an official matter and that personal emotions
must not be involved in it. Until he is sure that he is
going to get what he wants, he insists that he wants
nothing at all and that his duty is not his pleasure: "I am
perfectly resolved to return [to Ireland] as soon as I have
done my Commission whether it succeeds or no I neer
went to Engd with so little desire in my life". This is
not just a reassurance to the ladies he has left behind,

nor is it a declaration of preference for life in Ireland.
It is the careful statement of a haughty man who has
been disappointed before and, because disappointment
is to him the same thing as insult, is determined not to
be disappointed again: he has left a burrow behind him
in Ireland and will merely return to it with a polite
shrug if either his merits or his mission are treated with
neglect. This does not mean that he will retire at the first
rebuff, for he is both too strong-minded and too intelligent to do that. It means simply that if the incoming
Tory ministry treat him as the outgoing Whigs did, he
has a dignified line of retreat and ample room for quiet
disdain. "We shall have a strange winter here", he writes,
"between the struggles of a cunning provoked discarded
party, and the triumphs of one in power; of both of
which I shall be an indifferent spectator, and return very
peaceably to Ireland. . . ."

This guarded approach is characteristic of Swift, and
we may see behind it the thin-skinned aspirant whose
ambitiousness always coincides with a horror of being
affronted. It is the business of a powerful man who is
approached by such a one to respond with infinite tact-
fulness and extreme courtesy: only in this way can he
hope to disarm a potential enemy and make him, instead,
a devoted ally. This is just what Harley did—and by doing
so provides us with the chance to see how quickly Swift's
attitude could shift from one extreme to another. Used
"like a Lord" at that first interview, he not only laid down
his pride but admitted gladly in that evening's instalment
of the *Journal* that he, a minor figure, had been greatly
favoured by a very great one. "All this is odd and comical, if you consider him and me. He knew my Christian
name very well. . . . He charged me to come to him
often: I . . . desired I might have leave to come at his
levee; which he immediately refused, and said, That was
not a place for friends to come to". The prettiness of the
compliment pleased Swift immensely.

"He knew my Christian name very well". But Harley knew much more than that. He knew the story of Swift's Cavalier grandfather. He could tell Swift "that he had among his Father's (Sr. Edward Harley's) Papers severall letters from Mr. Thomas Swift" and he promised that Swift should have them if he would come to Brampton Bryan. As their friendship grew, Harley became fond of teasing Swift, and his favourite way of doing so was to address him as "Dr. Thomas Swift". Biographers have assumed that this nickname derived from Swift's cousin, the Rev. Thomas Swift of Puttenham, who was rumoured to be the "real" author of *A Tale of a Tub*. That explanation may be correct, but it is just as likely that when Harley came to know his man, he was amused to see in that pugnacious High Church face the characteristics of his grandfather's enemy, the Vicar of Goodrich. We enjoy history most when it makes small concessions to romance.

Yet, apart from this romantic element, the friendship of the two grandsons is of some historical interest. They meet at an agreed point, but each has reached that point by a different road. The Puritan of Brampton Bryan has been gradually edged into the position of a Church of England Tory by a Whig party that has become too warlike and Radical to suit his preference for peace and moderation. These Whigs look to the Dissenters for the popular support that will maintain their power, and by doing so they push the old-fashioned Puritan towards the side of Church and Crown. Here he meets the Cavalier's grandson, most of whose opinions are drawn from the history of the Civil War and whose personal inclination is to his grandfather's world. Yet, though one grandson has moved and one has remained stock still, history is engaged in circumventing both of them. They regard themselves as "moderate" men; they see their common ground as one on which all reasonable persons will be prepared to stand in order to prevent the disruptions of faction. But their attitude is moderate and reasonable only to them. The Dissenter cannot regard as "moderate" a ministry that denies him his civil rights, and the extreme Tory cannot regard as "reasonable" a ministry that keeps him out of office, placates the Whig enemy and seeks unity in affiliation. Thus no old division is healed when the grandsons find common ground, for they do so only at the very moment when the faction they deplore is about to grow into the approved form of democratic government. Much of the interest we find in the history of these years comes from watching the ideal of a limited unity yielding to the juster but more degraded practice of eternal division. Much of the sadness and anger that we find in Swift's later life arises not only from the death of the old ideal but from the brutish uglinesses that were a prologue to the two-party system of modern democracy.

＊   ＊   ＊

Swift's mission on behalf of the Church of Ireland succeeded as soon as he met Harley, but the Irish bishops could not be expected to know this. It took time for Harley's promise to take documentary form, and the bishops began to think that their ambassador had failed. They petitioned the Duke of Ormond, the incoming Lord-Lieutenant, to take over the mission, with the result that the public credit due to Swift went eventually to the Duke instead. ". . . the baseness of those bishops makes me love Ireland less than I did . . ." Swift wrote in the *Journal*, "but I have other things to mind, and of much greater importance . . . with a new ministry, who consider me a little more than Irish bishops do".

We note this with interest because it means that the affront to dignity that Swift had prepared himself to receive in England, came instead from the country into which he had prepared to retreat. The *Journal* lets us observe the interesting manner in which Swift put both countries on trial for his affections, the test in each case being that of attention and recognition. The early pages

of the *Journal* ask repeatedly what response Ireland is
making to her ambassador's various successes: what
do they say in Dublin of *Sid Hamet's Rod*; have they
"smoakt" the author of the *Shower*; "Do they know anything in Ireland of my greatness among the Tories?"

But no response seems to come from Ireland; only an
ignorant silence. Even the Archbishop of Dublin can
show no better gratitude to his successful ambassador
than to urge him to make hay for himself while the sun
shines. We understand better why Ireland was to seem
an exile to Swift if we compare that country's coldness to
him with the warmth he received from all sorts of great
persons in England. Ireland paid no attention to him at
all; in England, they brought him butter in a lordly dish.
Thereafter, only in moments of weariness or fear did he
dream of his willows at Laracor and long to walk again
through the Irish fields.

And as we read him, we accustom ourselves to his
characteristic swings—to his contempt on one page for
Irish "ingratitude" and his nervousness and vexation on
the next respecting his prospects in England. Both feelings are perfectly sincere: the philosopher who assures
the Archbishop that he has been content in Ireland with
"a scurvy acre of ground" is quite understandably the
same man as the hard-working politician who tells his
good friend Lord Peterborough: "My ambition is to live
in England, and with a competency to support me with
honour". One notes, too, that only once in the three years
of the *Journal* is he deeply angry with Hester Johnson:
this is when she has asked him if there is truth in the
report that he is to be Dean of Wells. The very mention
of such splendid preferment strikes him as painfully
tactless, and he answers sharply: "I had yr N. 32 at
Windsor. I just read it, and immediately sealed it up
again, and shall read it no more this twelve-month at
least. . . ."

Two things must be noted about this man who is so

cautious in his approaches and so sensitive to other
people's opinions. One is his readiness to be impressed
by the virtues of others and honour them with the praise
and gratitude that he liked to receive himself. In Robert
Harley, who was soon to be ennobled as 1st Earl of
Oxford and Mortimer, Swift found a man who was at
least his equal in learning and a high example of courage and good nature unspoilt by the grandeur of power.
In Harley's compeer, Henry St. John, the future Viscount
Bolingbroke, he found a "hero" that astonished him—a
rash, mercurial genius who had been Secretary of War at
only twenty-eight* and was now, at thirty-two, Secretary
of State and architect of the Treaty of Utrecht. This
young man—"the greatest young man I ever knew"—took
Swift by storm: he had not before met a man who would
suddenly disappear from a stroll in the Mall to chase
after a wench and yet "drudge all through the night in
his office like a common clerk" and "tomorrow be at the
cabinet with the Queen. . . ." How small and pompous,
by comparison, Sir William Temple seemed, who made
"such a splutter about being secretary of state at fifty-
five"! And how small and ignorant the young Swift, who
had walked in awe of Temple and suffered from his
"coldness"! At forty-three Swift was meeting worldly
greatness in its nicest form—a greatness that can afford
to laugh, to relax and almost to dispense with snobbery.
Those who are invited to share this carefree tableland
cannot fail to shed much of their own pride and to feel
exultation in having reached that zenith where a simplicity of manners and a naturalness of behaviour make

* After that he "retired" from political life to become a rustic
philosopher, and a friend wrote the following inscription for his
summer-house:
> From business and the noisy world retir'd,
> Nor vex'd by love, nor by ambition fir'd;
> Gently I wait the call of Charon's boat,
> Still drinking like a fish, and—like a stoat.

These lines pained the young man ("He swore to me that he could
hardly bear the jest . . ."), but they were a great delight to Swift.

stiffness and vanity look vulgar and petty. In truth, outside Swift's company both Harley and St. John pursued
pomps and vanities of the lordliest kind, and the cynic
might argue that their unbuttoned manner with Swift
was simply their way of resting their feet. Be that as it
may, they convinced him that the plainness and unaf-
fectedness he cherishèd so much were to be found at the
top of the tree: life with ministers who, for all their
"mighty difficulties" were "as easy and disengaged as
schoolboys on a holiday" quite ruined him for tolerating
lesser men.

The second thing we must note about Swift's relations
with these two is that though he loved them and was
proud of the affection they showed him, he never hesi-
tated to speak his mind to them and, on occasion, rebuke
them sharply. Swift, as Moriarty says, stepped into the
Tory party as "the adviser of the nation's chosen states-
men"—a self-appointment that entirely satisfied his tu-
torial tendencies. When Harley, still not understanding
that this was to be the tone of the relationship, sent him
a bank-bill of fifty pounds for services rendered, he not
only got it back immediately but was given to understand
that such an insult would be unpardonable if it were
repeated. With St. John, Swift was not only mindful of
his own pride but merciless to St. John's. When the Secretary of State (he seems to have been suffering from a
hangover) addressed Swift one day with coldness and
reserve he got the most startling rating: ". . . and one
thing I warned him of, Never to appear cold to me, for
I would not be treated like a schoolboy; that I had felt
too much of that in my life already (meaning from Sir
William Temple); that I expected every great minister,
who honoured me with his acquaintance, if he heard or
saw anything to my disadvantage, would let me know
in plain words, and not put me in pain to guess by the
change or coldness of his countenance or behaviour; for it
was what I would hardly bear from a crowned head. . . .

He took [it] all right; said, I had reason, vowed nothing ailed him but sitting up whole nights at business, and one night at drinking. . . ."

Once the desired relationship had been established, it never changed, except insofar as it grew stronger. We hear much of Swift's succumbing to the flattery of the great and of his being duped or ignored in matters of importance: "He was employed, not trusted", says Orrery, "and at the same time that he imagined himself a subtil diver, who dextrously shot down into the profoundest regions of politics, he was suffered only to sound the shallows nearest the shore, and was scarce admitted to descend below the froth at the top. Perhaps the deeper bottoms were too muddy for his inspection". But the point of interest for us is not the great men's deviousness with Swift, but Swift's honesty with them. To obtain Queen Anne's Bounty for Ireland was a light task; the work of speaking for the ministry in the *Examiner* was more a pleasure than a test of character. The courage and stature were shown, as Swift knew, in risking his friendship with the great by trying to impose his own principles upon them. If they kept much from him, he kept nothing from them, and his candour, as Orrery readily agrees, must always "redound to the honour of Dr. Swift: . . . He may have been carried away by inconsiderate passion, but he was not to be swayed by deliberate evil. He may have erred in judgment, but he was upright in intention. The welfare and prosperity of these kingdoms were the constant aim of his politics, and the immediate subject of his thoughts and writings".

"Inconsiderate passion" is undoubtedly the character-istic that makes it absurd for Swift to be seen as a practising proponent of the "middle way". The strength of his principles undoes the principles themselves; the vehemence of his hatred of "deliberate evil" leads him repeatedly both to see it where it is not present or, when he has convinced himself of its absence, not to allow

himself to see the least tincture of it. He tries constantly
to maintain a judicious equanimity, but "inconsiderate
passion" makes this impossible, driving him again and
again to inordinate affection or excessive indignation.
When his feelings are aroused, for better or for worse,
his judgement loses all balance and sobriety, and he
responds to both people and personal predicaments with
violence. We must learn to accept him as one who could
struggle with infinite patience and common sense to
check the inconsiderate passions of others but, at decisive
moments in his own life, could gallop into self-destruc-
tion with incredible recklessness and entire absence of
self-control.

If we deplore the destructiveness we must still, as
Orrery says, admire the constructive vigour of the patriotism. Swift's chief importance to the Tories was as their
spokesman and propagandist, but he himself put as his
first duty the task of turning their factiousness into
brotherhood. And this, we may say flatly, was not merely
because of the personal fear he often felt for his own
safety, should the ministry fall apart and be succeeded
by its enemies. His principles were much stronger than
his fears: he saw it as his plain duty to do everything he
could to hold his friends together. His instructions to
the great were short and unpolitical: they must love one
another. When he voiced this opinion to his dear friend
Peterborough, the nobleman replied that he must be out
of his mind and dreaming of a "golden age. How came
you to frame a system—in the time which we live in—to
govern the world by love?"

Swift admitted that when he spoke of love as the base
of political unity he did so with a smile—"between jest
and earnest", as he put it to Archbishop King. But there
is no doubt that he believed it, and for some time after
he arrived in England he rejoiced to be able to say of
the leading ministers: "I think they entirely love one another". Nor, when the ideal of love became absurd, as it

did very soon, did he ever stop struggling to impose the
decency of brotherhood on the bickering ministers. And
if he had not done so, we may add, the respect they had
for him would have been short-lived. Swift's power to
guide the course of politics was limited; the marvel is that
he was allowed to impose any guidance at all—to repri-
mand ministers, to tutor them in their best interests, to
remind them unceasingly of their proper duties. We are
so conscious of what they did behind his back that we
hardly notice how much he succeeded to their faces,
although we know very well that when he returned at
last to Ireland he was summoned back almost immediately as the only man who might yet pull together a
ministry that was breaking into pieces at last.

Swift knew very well how restricted his powers were:
he knew equally well that his influence was great and
could be put to good use. He used his influence exactly
as he used his money, setting a handsome part of it aside
for charitable purposes: the extraordinary success he had
in soliciting for others is the strongest evidence of the
strength of his position in the Ministry. Those who came
to Swift for help began with the ministers themselves,
who used him as their peacemaker: "For", said Harcourt,
the Lord Keeper, "Dr. Swift is not only all our favourite,
but our governor". It continued with the great men of
the day right down to the smallest and poorest of the
Queen's subjects. Swift was engaged by the Earl of
Abercorn, fantastic as it may seem, to obtain from Louis
XV the French dukedom which belonged to Abercorn by
hereditary right. At the other end of the scale, he sought
votes for Pompey, the Negro footman, who wanted to be
Leader in the "House of Commons" which the footmen
had set up in grave imitation of their masters. Between
these two frolicsome extremes we find a ceaseless flow of
honest, deserving cases—poverty-stricken parsons, minor
clerks, soldiers struggling to obtain commissions which
they cannot afford to buy, clerks of the customs and a

host of literary nonentities—"I am plagued with bad Authors, Verse and Prose, who send me their Books and Poems; the vilest Trash I ever saw. . . ." A few of these struggling solicitors made the dreadful mistake of offering Swift bribes: that is the last we hear of them—though it is pleasing to read, because virtue is nicer when it is not perfect, that the brace of wild-fowl sent by a suppliant poet ("te Rogue should have kept te Wings at least for his Muse . . .") was so plump that Swift, after sternly giving the birds away, popped round to dinner with the man he gave them to and sampled a slice of the bribe. Some of Swift's solicitations were quickly achieved, but others demanded months of his scrupulous attention; and there is one case with which he struggled for a year and a half before he succeeded. His attempted services to literary men involved almost every important writer in England except Defoe, and most of the writers he tried to help were of the other party, and more his enemies than his friends. "I have taken more pains", he writes in the *Journal*, "to recommend the Whig Witts to te Favour & Mercy of te Ministers than any other People. Steel I have kept in his Place; Congreve I have got to be used kindly and secured. Row I have recommended, and got a Promise of a Place; Philips I should certainly have provided for if he had not run Party-mad & made me withdraw my Recommendation; and I sett Addison so right at first that he might have been employed; and have partly secured him te Place he has. . . ." Here Swift is writing his own testimonial: we may test it by putting next to it the evidence of his Whig enemy, Bishop Kennett, who has left us a first-rate eye-witness account of Swift at his highest moment of worldly glory. The scene is Windsor; the date, 1713.

Dr. Swift came into the coffee-house, and had a bow from everybody but me. When I came to the ante-chamber to wait before prayers, Dr. Swift was the principal man of talk and business, and acted as a Master of Requests. He was soliciting

the Earl of Arran to speak to his brother the Duke of Ormond,
to get a chaplain's place established in the garrison of Hull
for Mr. Fiddes, a clergyman in that neighbourhood, who had
lately been in gaol, and published sermons to pay fees. He
was promising Mr. Thorold to undertake with my Lord
Treasurer, that, according to his petition, he should obtain
a salary of two hundred pounds per annum as Minister of
the English Church at Rotterdam. He stopped F. Gwynn,
Esq., going in with the red bag to the Queen, and told him
aloud that he had something to say to him from my Lord
Treasurer. He talked with the son of Dr. Davenant to be sent
abroad, and took out his pocket-book and wrote down several
things, as memoranda, to do for him. He turned to the fire,
and took out his gold watch, and telling him the time of day,
complained it was very late. A gentleman said he was too
fast. "How can I help it", says the Doctor, "if the courtiers
give me a watch that won't go right?" Then he instructed a
young nobleman, that the best poet in England was Mr. Pope
(a Papist), who had begun a translation of Homer into English verse, for which he must have them all subscribe. "For",
says he, "the author shall not begin to print till I have a
thousand guineas for him". Lord Treasurer, after leaving the
Queen, came through the room, beckoning Dr. Swift to follow
him; both went off just before prayers.

As a study of character in action—which is the only
real character, in the end—this description is not only
perfectly done but more important than any other por-
trayal of Swift ever written. It omits the extremes of
Swift's character—the soft-heartedness at one end, the
violent anger at the other—but this need not disturb us,
because Swift is too apt to be seen entirely in terms of
those extremes: he is never melancholy, but he is heart-
rent; he is never annoyed or chilly, but must always be
"thrown into a fury" or "driven to violent rage". The
Bishop shows him in all the easy sobriety in which he
passed the happier parts of his life, and yet the very
plainness of his picture magnifies our vision most use-
fully.

We are shown a man who is engaged in excellent work but is not entirely the more attractive for it. The ease of movement and the naturalness suggest, at least to the enemy, an underlying pomposity; the charity is not only lordly but rather offensive. We get the impression of superiority as much as benevolence, and we understand very well both why Swift was piqued so easily and why those to whom he extended a warm hand so often found it cold and drew away. "It is my delight to do good offices for those who want and deserve them", he writes to the ladies at this time: Bishop Kennett helps to remind us of a blindness that accompanied this—a failure to understand that a giver's delight imposes dutiful obligations on the recipients. Acutely sensitive in matters concerning his own independence, he seems not to care about the independence of others: the frankness we admire so much in him contains a good measure of personal vanity. We are not surprised to learn that such vanity made him unpopular—and we are relieved to know that many men were big enough to dismiss it as superficial or regard it as purely comical. We have, for instance, the Duke of Hamilton, "who must needs be witty" and, when the Doctor moves gravely upstairs, falls obsequiously to the rear and follows him up, carrying the end of his cassock like a royal train.

There was, then, we see, two sorts of relationship demanded by Swift. Where the mighty were concerned, he demanded the highest respect for himself. "I am so proud I make all the lords come up to me", he says, and to rub it in he loves "to turn from a Lord to te meanest of my Aquaintance". But where he himself was the lord, he demanded subservience and dependency, and when both sorts of demand were met he was the happiest of men, for his vanity was then fed at both ends, and the rewards of charitable behaviour ran with the triumphs of successful ambition. But those who regarded themselves simply as his equals found no place for themselves in such a scheme; nor did any place exist. They were neither Brobdignagians, who could bow low to Swift, nor Lilliputians, who could stare up at the sun of his countenance. They were men who asked only for personal independence and dignity and who, like Swift himself, preferred these to tactless benefactions. Steele, indeed, preferred not to recognize Swift as a benefactor at all: he liked to stand on his own feet, and fight his own battles with the Tory ministry and, when they retained him in one of his offices, feel that they had done so not because Swift had spoken up for him but because the ministry thought it good politics to placate him. This is vanity of a sort—but a sort for which we have some sympathy: Swift's sort, which feeds on gratitude, is displeasing to our sense of dignity.

To state the case this way is to state it at its worst—to allow the enemy to present the grounds for his dislike of Swift. This does no harm, provided we note how the same characteristics looked to men who knew Swift much better than Bishop Kennett did. Addison could be "cold and dry" when he and Swift were at loggerheads, but their mutual respect and affection made their differences seem trifling. Men of the kindest and best character, such as Bishop Berkeley and Dr. Arbuthnot, never found Swift pompous but always thought him warm-hearted, honest and good: "one of the best natured and agreeable men in the world" was Berkeley's verdict. Perhaps, then, the most we may assert is that Swift would not have said with Lamb: "The greatest pleasure I know, is to do a good action by stealth, and to have it found out by accident". Swift loved to give his help openly and to receive gratitude for it with equal frankness. His generosity was inseparable from his masterliness; he loved dearly to make small men bigger and know that the resulting handiwork was his own. His strongest and most paternal affection was aroused when such people acknowledged with a full heart the lordship of their maker.

Of these, "little Harrison" is a perfect and pathetic example. Son of a bawd, he was discovered by Swift in London in 1710 and put by him to writing *Tatlers*. He did this badly, so Swift steered him into diplomacy instead and obtained for him "te prettyest Post in Europe for a young gentleman"—Queen's Secretary at the Hague, with a salary of £1,000 a year. Harrison's last letter to Swift from the Hague ends with the sort of words that Swift loved best:

I beg, dear Sir, the continuance of your kind care and inspection over me; and that you would in all respects command, reprove, or instruct me as a father; for I protest to you, Sir, I do, and ever shall, honour and regard you with the affection of a son.

The sudden death of this affectionate young man gave great pain to Swift. He was "te little Brat; my own Creature"; "no loss ever grieved me so much" and "I shall never have courage again to care for making anybody's Fortune". Twenty years later, the death of Hester Johnson was to repeat, in greater depth, the same painful wound; for she, more than anyone, was Swift's "own Creature". All Swift's griefs were those of a father; all his anger at ingratitude was a father's, as was all his detestation of disobedience. He loved best where he governed most: what is the Irish patriot but the father of his children?

* * *

The charm of the *Journal to Stella* is manifold; but the romance that fills it is not that of love but that of the theatre. It is the book of a man who is on a big stage that cannot be seen by his audience: through his pen-pictures, the distant ladies see the bright, changing sets and side-scenes, the whole cast of actors, great and small. They hear snatches of the actual dialogues; each turn of the plot is recounted and explained to them: all this is their consolation for being unable to gain admission to

the theatre itself—and it is also, of course, the actor's
justification for not having stayed at home with them.
Both to the ladies and to us the principal character is
Swift himself, and he spares no pains to project his image
in all its movements and emotions from sunrise to sunset.
As with most of us, Swift's image is not a single one. He
has a gay, unbuttoned self whom he usually calls "pdfr"
and an *alter ego* known as "t'other I", who does the
serious business of attending cabinets, justifying Tory
policy, and so on: we soon get used to seeing "pdfr" and
"t'other I" taking turns, in spirit, to hold the stage and
write the *Journal*; between them they ring changes all
the way from farcical nonsense to tragedy. "pdfr" is, of
course, the homelier of the two, author of the "little language", purveyor of most of the sentiment and all the
mimicry. We live with him in his plain lodgings; we
know where his bed stands and where the fireplace is;
we get to know his "shaving days"; we go for his walks
with him, and when he has snuffed his candle at night we
hear with him the watchman crying "Paaaaast twelvvve
o'clock". The cries of London wake him in the morning—
"Rrrare Chelsea Buns!", "Cabbages and Savoys!" ("I wish
his largest Cabbage was sticking in his throat")—and
we rise and dress with him, knowing nearly every day
how much of his bushel of coal is left, what he must pay
for firing, and whether the temperature is sapping his
purse or putting him in a stew. Swift took great pride
in the fact that from these ordinary surroundings he
walked to the rooms of State in Westminster, returning
at night to the light of a single candle and, on wintry
days, the frozen water in the cage of his manservant's
linnet: his dignity was only the greater for the simplicity
in which it grew. To the door of his lodgings came a
stream of suppliants; soon, he had trained his servant
Patrick to be as clever as Harley's famous porter in denying that his master was at home. Patrick is an important
character in the *Journal* and sheds much light on the

character of his master. Feckless, wilful and frequently drunk, he tries Swift's patience for two long years: if servants write testimonials for their masters, Patrick's for Swift speaks highly of his master's goodness.

The London that Swift shows us is one that makes our own seem infinitely rude and ugly. It is a city in which business and hay-making are pursued together: the laws of the countryside are evident not only in dunghills, mud, dust and surface sewerage but in the fresh water of the Thames and the goodness of the air. In night-gown and slippers Swift pads down to the riverside on hot evenings and bathes naked except for a napkin—this, oddly enough, he binds round his head. In the hot days, "poor little pdfr sweats mightily" as he walks to cabinet meetings—and suddenly we see again, to our surprise, the rotund Swift of the Orrery frontispiece, the short, Churchillian man. What this man lives on, we cannot say: he has precious little money and can afford only the most ordinary wig. He hardly ever buys his own dinner, fortunately: when he is not eating at Harley's or St. John's table he has an abundance of hostesses to choose from and carries us with him into half the great houses of London. The two ladies in Ireland are not told that the chief of these hostesses, Mrs. Vanhomrigh, has a young daughter with whom Swift is becoming more and more deeply involved; instead, every effort is made to mention the mother as often as possible so as not to draw attention to the daughter: this is embarrassed deceit trying its best to pretend to honesty. But there is no need for subterfuge outside the Vanhomrigh household, and all the London ladies are shown vying with one another to capture the Doctor—the more so because he is a choosy guest and visits no house of which he does not approve. He entertains them with his conversation, supervises their card-games, lectures them and provokes them: the bolder ones enjoy teasing the lion and think of tricks to play on him. His hat is stolen and held out of the win-

dow; a hand reaches out from the adjoining house, takes
the hat and passes it on to the next house: when Swift at
last looks out of the window for his hat, it is on a window
spike five doors away, and to get it back he must pay a
call at a house full of elderly "beldames". Some women
had a very happy knack at handling Dr. Swift: if they
were never able to twist him round their little finger,
they were certainly able to twist his tail round it, and he
was never happier than when they were doing so. The
men he was fondest of were also very good at "rallying"
the Doctor, particularly when he was on his high horse
or trying to govern England too despotically. Driving to
Windsor with St. John, the Doctor refused to miss his
dinner, which he liked having punctually at 2 P.M. So the
Secretary of State halted the carriage at Brentford,
ordered a vast dinner ("the two of us ate roast beef like
Dragons")—and left Swift to pay the bill. "I [had] only
designed to eat a bit of bread and butter", Swift complains in the *Journal*, adding: "I don't like such jesting,
yet I was mightily pleased with it too".

This is a very nice admission on "pdfr's" part: we feel,
at moments, that there was something of Mr. Pooter at
the Mansion House ball in Dr. Swift at the court of
Queen Anne.

Swift's rules of decorum were very strict, but it is not
easy to explain how he applied them in practice. We find
it odd that a man who wrote very grossly should make
the pure court of Charles I his model of social intercourse
and march from the room when the conversation of
politicians became indecent ("I give no man liberty to
swear or talk b——dy.") We are puzzled when Mrs. Long,
the toast of the Kit-Kat Club and a great favourite of
Swift's, is banished for writing him a letter with "no less
than two nasty jests in it with dashes to suppose them":
we find exactly such jests and dashes in the *Journal* itself.
Perhaps, in vulgarity as in charity, Swift was an insensitive giver but a hypersensitive receiver. Perhaps he felt

he could allow "pdfr" more latitude than "t'other I" could accept from others. Certainly, his behaviour reminds us that nothing in a person is harder to understand exactly than his capacity to be shocked and that we must accept with a tolerant shrug the angry blush with which the gunman responds to any denigration of motherhood.

Swift has other rules of decorum that seem to us one-sided. Where propaganda is concerned, he believes in liberty for himself and suppression for his enemies: he hates the Lord Chief Justice, who cannot agree that what Swift writes is always patriotic but that what Swift's foes write is usually "libel" and "treason". Swift's view is unacceptable today, but it is not at all difficult to understand. It is a natural view to take when the failure of a Ministry is punished by imprisonment and impeachment. In such a world those who are "out" are classed as "rogues": only those who are "in" can be regarded as loyal and respectable enough to enjoy freedom of speech. In his London years Swift enjoyed the liberty of Tory power. When the Whigs came in, he took his turn as an outcast scoundrel. Once politics ceased to be a matter of life and death, this simple system became impractical.

Most of the rules which we see Swift applying in the *Journal* are based, for better or worse, on simple grounds of firm principle. We see him intervening to prevent the pardoning of a man who has been condemned to hang for raping a prostitute. The Under-Secretary of State believes that the character of the woman justifies the pardoning of the man. But Swift does not. "What! must a woman be ravished because she is a whore?" he demands. We note here the rightness of the principle—but we note, too, that the power to pardon exists precisely to prevent principle from being carried too far.

The remaining rules of Swift come under the same head as that which he laid down for prose: "Proper Words in Proper Places is the True Definition of a Style". The most illustrative example of this is shown in his attempt to set up an academy to discipline the whole English language. The scheme for this is sketched out in the only work that Swift signed with his own name: *A Proposal for Correcting, Improving and Ascertaining the English Tongue (1712)*. This interesting paper is like a translation into lingual terms of Swift's principal attitude to life itself and shows us clearly that unity of character which framed his many diverse expressions. The English language, he tells us, has suffered in the same way as the English body politic. Cromwell's "Usurpation" struck it at the very moment when it was achieving decency and elegance under Charles I and flooded it with "an Infusion of Enthusiastick Jargon". In succeeding years, "Dunces of Figure" followed "the Affectation . . . to introduce and multiply *Cant* Words, which is the most ruinous corruption in any language". Fashion, in the shape of "illiterate Court-Fops, half-witted Poets, and University-Boys", introduced the monstrous abbreviations (for example, *mob* for *mobile*) that are helping to change the language so greatly that posterity will be unable to understand the proper speech and writing of the time of Queen Anne. Swift does not deny that a living language must grow, at least to some extent, but he can see "no absolute Necessity why any Language should be perpetually changing": moreover, if English were "once refined to a certain Standard, perhaps there might be ways to fix it forever. . . ." It is impossible to read these phrases without recognizing how exactly they repeat, in their particular context, Swift's general attitude to history and human behaviour. English prose simply takes its place alongside religion, politics and manners: to "fix it forever" despite fashion, faction and fanaticism is the essential alternative to an anarchical vocabulary and syntax answerable to nothing but individual whim— "Every Man His own Carver".

This, of course, is "t'other I" speaking. "pdfr" knows that there is a proper place for improper words, and when he climbs into bed with nightcap and candle, he passes on to the ladies by night the words that "t'other I" has condemned by day. The cant and jargon come rolling out in a happy stream—even *pozz* and *bamboozle*, which "t'other I" has singled out for special condemnation, take their place in the *Journal*. They march very contentedly with such pretty conceits of "pdfr's" own inventing as "Will she pass in a crowd? Will she make a figure in a country church?" And when the epistle to his "hunny" is finished, "pdfr" pops it in the post "with my own fair hands". But he is careful not to enclose the handkerchiefs he has bought for the ladies. They "will be put in some friend's pocket, not to pay custom".

*   *   *

The final thing the *Journal* has to tell us is information about the author in his profession as clergyman. We find, as might be expected, that where his friends and admirers are concerned there are no difficulties of recognition involved: the politician, the wit, the amusing friend are seen as part of the Doctor of Divinity. This is not merely because the Doctor demands extreme respect for the cloth, but also because he behaves like a clergyman at those crucial moments when politics and social intercourse are interrupted violently by personal tragedies. When the Duke of Hamilton, the "witty" bearer of the Doctor's train, is killed in a duel Swift arrives immediately to soothe the desperate widow and order her into a backroom where she will not be "tortured with te noise of te Grubstreet Screamers, mention[ing] her Husbands murder to her Ears". When Ormond loses his favourite daughter Swift, to whom she was also "my greatest favourite", is the family's principal consoler: finding on one of his visits the bereaved mother and sister weeping together, he "chid them" and sent them to separate rooms, explaining in the *Journal* that "there is something of Farce in all those Mournings let them be ever so serious. People will pretend to grieve more than they really do, and that takes off from their true Grief". Both these incidents show nicely the blend of pity and common sense that marks the true cleric.

The *Journal* tells us much of his ministering to the sick and the aged—the hours he gave to them, the attention he gave to their affairs. It tells us, too, that there were moments when he felt that dreadful conviction of the wretchedness of existence that grew on him so terribly in his last years. "I hate life when I think it exposed to such accidents", he writes, on the death of Ormond's daughter, "and to see so many thousand wretches burthening te Earth while such as her dye, makes me think God did never intend Life for a Blessing". Later, he was to repeat this cry more furiously; but never, even at the worst moments of his life, did it cause him to feel anything remotely resembling religious doubts.

These doubts were felt by his enemies—and perhaps by all who never knew him intimately. And such doubts, in their turn, were crucial to Swift's career: they are the factor that make us feel, as we read the *Journal*, how much personal misery and disappointment is building up below the surface of this cheerful book. Swift could enable Queen Anne to enjoy the credit of extending her "bounty" to the Church of Ireland. He could persuade her, again through intermediaries, to build in London fifty new churches, to accommodate, then, a rising population and delight, now, the devotees of eighteenth-century architecture. Clergymen have been made bishops for much less than this, yet neither Swift nor his political friends were ever able to persuade the Queen that the clergyman from whom these services to religion originated had any religion himself. One might almost say that thanks to this stupid woman's horror of *A Tale of a Tub*, the writing of *Gulliver's Travels* was made possible, and that both books have done much to enhance her glory as queen of one of culture's greatest ages.

In the *Journal* Swift never once admits that his Queen would have nothing to do with him—that his place was always her ante-room and that though, on occasion, he might see her pass and bow to her with the rest, he was never presented to her, never preached before her, never received any sort of recognition from her. But the *Journal* also omits to state that the final responsibility for Swift's disappointment lay in his own "inconsiderate passion". The Duchess of Somerset, the Queen's Mistress of the Robes and closest confidante, happened most unfortunately to be one of the few women in England who also had a strong grudge against Dr. Swift. Years before, as literary executor to Sir William Temple, he had published documents that gave pain to the Duchess's family and caused her to describe him as "a man of no principle either of honour or religion". That this very woman should now have the Queen's ear and hold the power to decree Swift's future drove him to the worst extreme of panic and anger. Rather than wait to be humiliated by her veto, he characteristically precipitated it, and, in a violent lampoon, *The Windsor Prophecy*, so assaulted her honour, religion and principles as to make it impossible for her ever to think better of his own. " 'Tis an admirable good one and people are mad for it", said Swift of the lampoon that was to be his ruin—and thereafter, he could always cite the Duchess as the "red-haired, murd'ring hag" who had driven him into exile. The most useful conclusion we can draw from this nasty episode is that when Swift was overcome by "inconsiderate passion" he was prepared not only to punish others but to press upon them a positive obligation to humble his pride and even ruin his life with a clear and contented conscience. Whether the Duchess ever forgave or forgot *The Windsor Prophecy*, we cannot say: Swift himself never forgave the Duchess, but did manage to forget *The Windsor Prophecy*. "I fancy I did not write (it)", he said, twenty years later.

The Deanery of St. Patrick's was granted him by his
friend the Duke of Ormond at Swift's own request: he
got it because it was the only office of dignity that was
not in the Queen's gift. This fundamental weakness in
Swift's position is what gives the *Journal* its recurrent
tone of alarm, apprehension and fear. Swift loves going
to court; he loves good conversation, intellectual ex-
changes, attractive women and frivolous pleasures—but
again and again they throw him back on a yearning for
substantial, well-founded things—for the solidities of
place, person and Nature as opposed to whimsical,
chanceful things that are governed by fashion, faction
and mere human impulse. Half-hidden behind both
"pdfr" and "t'other I" is an ordinary, worried soul that
sees these two fellows as mere actors in a charade—mere
"turns" that have no lasting substance. Gay or grave, they
pay off no debts, they provide no solidity, they chalk up
promise only of trouble and an unhappy end. It is this
anxious soul that suffers at night from dreams that he
finds absurd but cannot shake off: "the worst of dreams
is, that one wakes just in the humour they leave one".
Sickness, deprivation, threats of imprisonment in "a black
dungeon" are the substance of these dreams, and most
of them (there are nine in all) are full of alarms and
anxieties about Hester Johnson's condition and the
dreamer's precarious relations with her: in one, which
Swift dreams at the moment when his relations with Miss
Vanhomrigh are closest, Miss Johnson suddenly turns up
in London—though she assures him that "her stay will be
short". In another he is back in Ireland, when a message
comes suddenly from London demanding his immediate
appearance at a cabinet: what is he to do, for he has lost
every stitch of clothing and is walking the streets of
Dublin stark naked? This dream of finding himself in
Ireland shorn of all clothing is one that recurs "very
often": it foretells very accurately the future that awaits
him.

The further the *Journal* goes, the more we sympathize with the alarm and insecurity of the troubled dreamer. To reconcile the quarrelling leaders of the Tory party is a duty that not only becomes increasingly useless to them but increasingly dangerous for Swift. The more he commits himself to them, the less good he does to himself; the larger he looms in his role of spokesman and conciliator, the more he invites the punishment and revenge of his Whig enemies. Some of his biographers have written sarcastically about his feelings of panic, but it is hard to see why the prospect of being imprisoned in the Tower, as Harley was, could fail to frighten the bravest biographer. When Swift chose the Deanery of St. Patrick's as his reward and his security, he did not know that he was choosing simultaneously a place of permanent exile or that the safety he procured was to be also his punishment and his "black dungeon". To us the years to come are among the best of his life, but to him they were the long, relentless anti-climax to a short moment of magnificence.

PART THREE

"THIS IS TO WELCOME YOU to my neighbourhood . . ."
began the congratulatory letter from Archbishop
King—who did *not* desire at all to welcome Swift to his
neighbourhood and was at the same time assuring others
that the new Dean was none of his making. He went on
to tell Swift that a high duty awaited him at St. Patrick's
—the erection of a 120-foot spire atop the cathedral
steeple, "which kind of ornament is much wanting in
Dublin" and might, by Swift's provision of it, "give the
people there an advantageous notion of you". Everybody
is tactless from time to time, but the Archbishop's tact-
lessness in dealing with Swift was so nicely provocative
that it must always be denied the saving grace of stupidity and seen as an example of nimble clerical cattiness.
It recurs again and again in their fascinating correspondence and never fails of its intention—which is always to
exasperate Swift and goad him into strong, lengthy retorts: on receiving these the Archbishop then insists with
charming urbanity that he had never meant his remarks
to be taken seriously. Archbishop King deserves very
special study, because he is the only man who treated
Swift in this insolent manner and not only got away with
it but, reversing the usual rule, made himself seem the
headmaster (which, indeed, he was) and Swift seem the
stubborn boy. As sparring correspondents, they are a fine
pair to read—always at odds, always bargaining, always

stylish, always respectful—almost perfect enemies, in fact, until a common Irish patriotism unites them happily in the last years of the Archbishop's life.

In the present case the Archbishop's insincere congratulations and trivial advice intruded on the most painful and catastrophic moment of Swift's life. First and foremost, the catastrophe was of a sort we know very well: a man devotes the whole energy of his youth to the attainment of a fixed ambition and, having won what he sought triumphantly, finds that by accident or unexpected circumstances his victory is worthless. The *Journal to Stella* describes exactly the brilliant success of Swift's boyhood determination to be used like a lord and see his wit do service for a carriage and horses; for a few short years he exults in the pride and happiness of fulfilled desire, and then, with celerity and finality, is dismissed from the world of his triumphs by circumstances that are uncontrollable even by the strongest will. This happens to Swift when he is in the very prime of life and when his power to influence the course of affairs is at its zenith: the whole aim and purpose of his life is wrecked at the very moment of his obtaining it. History gives us numberless examples of this sort of personal catastrophe; it is one of the oldest stories in the world. And history tells us, too, that many of the strong-willed and energetic men to whom it happens do not accept it lying down: when the first shock is over they become what Swift became— a dangerous, relentless outlaw, obedient to no power and government but his own. England, moreover, had seen to it that this spirit of outlawry should be inevitable, for England had consigned Swift to live forever in the very place where he was most held in contempt and must feel with special acuteness the awfulness of his disaster. When he arrived for his installation he was hooted in the streets, and his Chapter, well primed by the Archbishop, received him with scorn, coldness and hostile resentment.

Numerous officials and clerical persons came to pay him complimentary visits which were in fact only cold, impersonal formalities—"all to the Dean and none to the Doctor", he told Miss Vanhomrigh: it is a sad little phrase. He went on: "I thought I should have died with discontent and was horribly melancholy while they were installing me; but it begins to wear off and change to dulness".

Dulness, at first, is indeed the word. The next few years of Swift's life are marked with the heaviness that afflicts a man who has courage enough to face great difficulties but no heart-felt impulse to do so. The work must be done, but to no interesting purpose; an unwanted position must be established and upheld, but only for the sake of dignity, personal security and the proper performing of necessary duties. Swift set about this work and did it successfully, settling stolidly into "the great house . . . which they say is mine", obtaining the respect and obedience of his hostile Chapter, out-thwarting the Archbishop, and organizing as practically as possible the unattractive elements that composed his exile. As the years passed, he began to raise a new spirit on this substantial beginning, but for a long time we see only the Dean who has ceased to be the Doctor—a functionary who is no longer a person, a dulled automaton who accepts a minor public office with the words "I have a mind to be at home, since the Queen has been pleased that Ireland should be my home". But this numbness was not absolute; it did not extend to an indifference as to the fate of his friends. For soon after Swift entered his Irish deanery, George I ascended the English throne, and one of the first acts of his first Whig ministry was to punish the principal enemies among the Tories and open the pork-barrel to the hungry Whigs. The very men that Swift loved and honoured most were impeached—his patron, Ormond; his "hero", St. John; the friend of his heart, Harley, who "distinguished and chose me above all other men while he was great". The closest associates of these ministers were marked down for cross-examination: there was the possibility that Swift himself would be called to London to be questioned with the rest. His complicity with the ministers had been no mere public association, for his first act when Harley fell had been to write to the disgraced Lord Treasurer and beg leave to fall in concert by retiring with him to Brampton Bryan: this he followed up with the so-called "Great Letter", which Harley received in the Tower, repeating plainly and passionately his devotion to the fallen minister. "I do not conceive myself obliged", he writes, "to regulate my opinions by the proceedings of a House of Lords or Commons; and therefore, however they may aquit themselves in your Lordship's case, I shall take the liberty of thinking and calling you, the ablest and faithfulest minister, and truest lover of your country that this age hath produced". And after likening the impeachment to a murderous attack that had been made on Harley by a Frenchman a few years before, he continued: "You were destined to both trials, and the same power which delivered you out of the paws of the lion and the bear will, I trust, deliver you out of the hands of the uncircumcised".

This letter must remind us that the characteristic that drove Swift to inordinate anger, suspicion and spite towards his enemies drove him equally to reckless defiance of caution and considerations of personal safety when his friends were in danger and his cause good. If we are shocked by his outbursts of vindictiveness, we must also be delighted by a letter to a prisoner in the Tower in which the mighty politicians responsible are dismissed as "the uncircumcised". The unjust passion, we are pleased to see, is as readily a just one; the leaning to ferocity inclines equally to bravery. Once we accept this as a simple truth about Swift, there is no need for us to run to extremes either of idolatry or denigration in summing him up: he himself will always provide words and actions that will justify both.

The "Great Letter" is also the moment in Swift's life when we feel most strongly the romantic loyalty and devotion of his Herefordshire grandfather, and it is strange indeed to think that if the Queen had been less obstinate, he could have returned to the family county as Bishop of Hereford, with Harley as a near neighbour— a final and apt reconciliation of grandsons. Instead, as we read Swift's letters to his separated friend, we content ourselves somewhat with feeling that the romantic chance to ally himself with the Minister was very pleasing to Swift; for there is consolation for personal distress in acting in the manner of the great patriots of Rome and Greece.

We may, however, think it curious that his friendship and loyalty to Ormond and St. John also continued as steadfastly as ever when these two avoided imprisonment by escaping to the Continent, where they joined the Old Pretender. We are not surprised that they should have done so, but we are surprised that Swift, who had repeatedly and sarcastically pooh-poohed the idea that the Tory leaders had any taint of Jacobitism, should not have felt that his two friends had betrayed his trust and made him look silly—offences which he usually regarded as unforgivable. That he did not take this attitude now merely shows how infinitely deeply he was distressed by what seemed to him the far more real betrayal of these men by their Whig enemies and their new king. We may charge Harley, St. John and Ormond with numerous personal failings, but whether we are Whig or Tory, we are not likely to suggest that the few years of Harley's government were in any way so corrupt and disgraceful as to warrant the impeaching of the principal ministers. The history books record injustices done to individual Whigs—among which we may include Swift's personal attacks on Godolphin, the Duchess of Marl-

borough and the Duchess of Somerset. But they tell us
nothing of gross sorts of legislation that inflicted suffering
on the population, apart from measures against the Dissenters which were thought up by Whigs themselves as a
device for making Harley unpopular. They show us why
Harley's artfulness, St. John's ambition and Swift's eloquence should have made them many enemies even
within their own party, but they tell us of no great
calamities following as consequences. Meanwhile, on the
side of prominent achievement, they record the long,
industrious negotiations that led to the Treaty of Utrecht,
and the continuance of national stability through years
of crisis and uncertainty.

The *obviousness* of this is what we must consider
when we try to understand Swift's horror at his friends'
impeachments and his inability to feel in any way out-
raged by the treasonable retort of two of them. He did
not approve their course: one of his letters indicates that
if he had thought he could get to England in time, he
would have done his best to dissuade Ormond from
flying to France. Nevertheless, it was his belief that but
for these "traitors", the new king would not have mounted
the throne of a relatively quiet and contented country,
nor would his new ministers have had the fortunate
opportunity to inherit the benefits accruing from the
stopping of a war that had lasted for over twenty years.
Swift never at any time admits to St. John's treason; indeed, we would think he was entirely insensitive to it but
for a letter in which Archbishop King spitefully draws his
attention to it in his usual friendly manner. But one may
suggest not only that he refused to see it as such but
even took a certain pleasure in what he deemed a well-
deserved retort to royal and national ingratitude. And it
was this ingratitude, not the behaviour of its victims, that
scarred his own feelings from this time on, as if he saw
in his own exile and that of his friends a repetition of
the boorish treatment that the factious Greeks and

Romans had inflicted on their great patriots. Lemuel Gulliver, in his phase of great physical magnitude, extinguishing the fires of royal Lilliput with his own urine, or towing away single-handed the whole fleet of the nation's enemies, is rewarded not merely with prudish enmity but with a plot to blind him while he sleeps: this giant represents no one person; he embodies the great leaders of a whole ministry and, beyond them, all mighty servants of small-minded, ungenerous states. But Gulliver belongs to the later period of Swift's refreshed belligerency; to gauge accurately his author's despondency of the moment we must read the various versions of his posthumously published *History of the Last Years of Queen Anne*. The dignity with which the fallen ministers' case is presented; the inordinate plainness of the language; the absence of any obvious bias, irony or sarcasm—all these serve, as Swift intended them to serve, less as an appeal to the living than as parts of a noble memorial or monument to which posterity could turn when it wanted to know the truth.

To the deep pain that Swift felt for the fate of his friends were added pains of a personal sort and a considerable amount of fear. His letters to and from his friends in England were opened and read by officials: one of these so-called Lord Justices was the Archbishop of Dublin himself, who, with one hand, forwarded Swift's intercepted letters to the Secretary of State and, with the other, wrote to assure Swift of his ever-friendly regard. But one is pleased to note that the dangers of the written word did nothing to make Swift play safe where he felt it his duty to console and encourage: he smuggled letters of exhortation and affection to Harley's son and the distressed wives of St. John and Ormond; and when we read the grateful answers of the two forlorn women, who were destined never to see their husbands again, we understand better than ever not only how much loyalty and friendship meant to Swift but why those who could

claim him as a friend trusted every word he spoke and
honoured him with life-long devotion and respect. This
high degree of trust, one must note, was absolutely insisted upon by Swift himself. One of the few men who
visited him as a friend after his installation as Dean was
the young Tory squire, Knightly Chetwode: the two out-
casts exchanged numerous letters over a period of many
years, and it is in one of the first of these that the young
man is enlightened as to what will be expected of him if
he is to rank as a friend. Whatever rumours reach
Chetwode's ears concerning remarks about him said to
have been dropped by Swift, he is not only to dismiss as
lies but take it for granted that Swift would speak only
good of him and dismiss from his presence as a "rude
beast" any visitor that spoke otherwise. "I would say thus
much to few men", Swift concludes: "Because generally
I expect to be trusted, and scorn to defend myself".

Of real friends Swift had virtually none in Ireland save
the two ladies and Esther Vanhomrigh. In Ireland there
were no teasing women to steal the Doctor's hat; no men
like his English "Brothers" to "rally" him and delight in
his conversation. Nothing ranked higher than friendship
in Swift's estimation; never had his life been richer in
friends than during the years of Harley's ministry. To be
separated from them so brutally was perhaps the worst
pain of all—"pray God forgive them", he wrote in later
years to St. John, "by whose indolence, neglect, or want
of friendship, I am reduced to live with twenty leagues
of salt water between your Lordship and me".

All this is summed up in the poem *In Sickness*, written
at that time and remarkable for its numb tone: Swift enjoyed a normal amount of self-pity, but expressed it
usually with a vigour and gusto that is quite absent
in these dull lines:

> 'Tis true,—then why should I repine,
> To see my Life so fast decline?
> But, why obscurely here alone?

Where I am neither lov'd nor known.
My State of Health none care to learn;
My Life is here no Soul's Concern.
And, those with whom I now converse,
Without a Tear will tend my Herse.
Remov'd from kind Arbuthnot's Aid,
Who knows his Art but not his Trade;
Preferring his Regard for me
Before his Credit or his Fee.
Some formal Visits, Looks, and Words,
What meer Humanity affords,
I meet perhaps from three or four,
From whom I once expected more;
Which those who tend the Sick for pay
Can act as decently as they.
But, no obliging, tender Friend
To help at my approaching End,
My Life is now a Burthen grown
To others, e'er it be my own.
    Ye formal Weepers for the Sick,
In your last Offices be quick:
And spare my absent Friends the Grief
To hear, yet give me no Relief;
Expir'd To-day, entomb'd To-morrow,
When known, will save a double Sorrow.

Yet the decisive thing about this period of Swift's life
is not only the situation in which he was put but the
steps he took to make sure that it would not get better.
The dryness of his private life—those formal, decanal
relationships—was encouraged by him to continue: he
wanted no repetition in Ireland of the intimacies which
he had loved in England.

As we have seen from the *Journal to Stella*, London
life had a sweetening and mollifying effect on Swift's
authoritative character: much of the rigour in his nature
fell away. Back in Ireland with neither the prestige of
power nor the pleasures of society, he set to work with
extreme grimness to build a new life that would defy

humiliation and disappointment. This life would centre
on a little, personal kingdom built on a base of clerical
authority, for just as "little Harrison's" death had shown
Swift the sad consequence of trying to make another's
career, so did the loss of his old friends make him swear
that he would never engage again in friendship. This
time, in place of friends he would have only obsequious
dependents, court favourites and selected jesters. Young
ladies and gentlemen who were prepared to accept the
Dean's teaching and discipline would be admitted to this
court, along with submissive minor clerics and awe-
inspired students. Harmless comedians such as Thomas
Sheridan, who needed but one rap over the knuckles to
teach him how far his jocularity could go, took the place
of the London "Brothers"; scholarship and high conversation were replaced with ribaldry, dog-Latin and childlike
buffoonery—"the most trifling amusements", as Swift
declares, "to divert the vexation of former thoughts, and
present objects". The Dean was absolute governor and
sole arbiter; he alone might decide the court *ton* and
define the limits within which it operated. Thanks to its
peculiar charter, the Deanery of St. Patrick's enjoyed rare
and unusual powers; by studying closely the exact nature
of these and insisting upon them to the letter, Swift
turned his cathedral and its precincts into a private
Vatican. When he rode forth into the outside world he
did so as a governor or viceroy, paced by a groom in
front and a valet behind. No longer a maker and shaper
of national policies, he became one that ordered the lives
of minions, ruling their studies, landscaping their gar-
dens, directing their health, habits and general behaviour:
provided they obeyed, he was genial, amusing and even
tolerant. When, with the passing of the years, the small
business men and shopkeepers of Dublin came to trust
the Dean and ask his advice, they were included as
humble subjects in his kingdom. All this was done with
the grimmest deliberation and most calculated deter-

mination. "If one cannot mend the public, one had better mend old shoes", Swift told St. John, and again and again until the end of his life declared his intention "to have noone about me that denies my authority" and to live the life of "a king among slaves".

The building of this glowering fortress is a far more remarkable work than the provision of a mere cathedral spire (it was left to Swift's successor to raise that unwanted ornament). But if it served Swift's purpose well enough, it also cost him dear. Nobody knew better how bad it is for kings to live among subservient courtiers, or how much bitterness and sense of absurdity in loneliness troubles a despot when he has closed the door on the last of his fools and slaves and is alone until next day with his own thoughts and memories. So it is that these years mark simultaneously the saddest and greatest alterations in Swift's life, yielding his best fiction, poems and pamphleteering, as well as his magnificent letters, but at the same time involving him in growing personal unhappiness and contempt for life. The same enormous will-power directed him for better and for worse—to a greater glory than he had ever won before and to a greater triviality. It drove him also to an almost frenzied independence: while he exulted in having made himself the unassailable "Captain Tom" of Ireland, he persisted in the belief that he was never secure from his enemies. Commending Pope for a political neutrality that won the poet admiration equally from Whig and Tory, he assured him fiercely that such coolness of temper could never be his own lot, for "I who am sunk under the prejudices of another education, and am every day persuading myself that a dagger is at my throat, a halter about my neck, or chains about my feet, all prepared by those in power, can never arrive at the serenity of mind you possess". Writing this in 1723, when his literary prowess seemed far more impressive to those in power than his political dangerousness, he was rebuked politely

by his friend Arbuthnot, who answered him: "By a para-
graph in yours to Mr. Pope, I find you are in the case of
the man, who held the whole night by a broom bush, and
found when daylight came, he was within two inches of
the ground. You do not seem to know how well you stand
with our great folks". But it is doubtful if Swift desired to
know. No "Captain Tom" likes to be persuaded that his
ferocity and hatred are largely wilful emotions that he
has encouraged because he regards them as essential
to his point of view.

It is possible that the maintaining of an unyielding
hatred was necessary for a more important reason—to
arm Swift against hoping too much that one day he
might obtain preferment in England. Had he been able
to dismiss this hope, it is possible that his life would
have had less of the mortification that grew with hope's
disappointments. Moreover, while hope remained, his
rigid, despotic regime was vulnerable to destruction by
his own hand: he might at any moment be tempted by
hope to chance his fortune in England and, failing, have
to retreat once more to Ireland with new wounds to his
pride and deeper disappointments. In fact, he yielded
to this temptation only once, when George II came to
the throne and Swift came to court and made his bow.
But there was to be no reprieve from the new king, nor
a new government of ministers tolerable to Swift: the
visit served no purpose but to humiliate the outlaw and
fill him with self-contempt for having exposed himself to
rebuff.

The difficult thing about these years is to assess them
soberly enough. The difficulty with Swift always is not
to find the right words but to escape having to eat them.
Thus, having stressed the despondency of these years, one
must go on to remember that it was the despondency
of one who declared himself "a stranger to the spleen"—
and this is borne out by his behaviour and his writings
even in his years of exile. Swift's will might impose on

him a life of severity, hatred and despotic control of
himself and his small empire, but his will was never
able to prevent him from relapsing into "pdfr's" natural
good humour and moments of happiness: this was well
known to that intelligent student of his character, Esther
Vanhomrigh. In the first three years of his exile he was
too dispirited to write either fiction or pamphlets, and
his poems were limited to a mere five: *In Sickness*, an ode
to the imprisoned Harley, a sour fable on the Scottish
Church, a Latin poem to Sheridan and a polite snub to
the same jester for allowing his wit to become offensive.
But by 1719 and 1720 Swift's spirits had risen again: his
first Irish pamphlet (*Proposal for the Universal Use of
Irish Manufactures*) had brought him back into politics,
the writing of *Gulliver's Travels* had begun and he was
producing a great variety of poems. It is these poems
that make us note the fact that when Swift's spirit was
roused, he was incapable of maintaining the grim despondency that his will enjoined. That gross assault on
the female and her cosmetics, *The Progress of Beauty*,
is simultaneous with the famous *The Progress of Poetry*,
that most endearing of hymns to the songsters of Grub
Street. Side by side with the sour political satires is *The
Description of an Irish feast*, Swift's admirable rendering
of a rowdy Irish ballad. The most we should say, therefore, of these early years of exile is that after first dulling
Swift's responses and sobering his temper, they soon provoked him into defiance of the dull, ignoble society in
which he was obliged to live. His letters and poems
suggest that this defiance took the form of seeing the
world and people in extreme terms, of looking with intense distaste on the general run of people and with
equally intense affection on a chosen few. Harley, in
Swift's eulogies, is scarcely statesman or politician; he is
a saint in a world of rogues. Harley's female equivalent,
or paragon among drabs, is Esther Vanhomrigh—who is
also our best guide not merely to Swift's state of mind

in the first ten years of his exile but to many of the rarer
features of his peculiar character.

*   *   *

Miss Vanhomrigh has tired badly under two centuries
of cross-examination. Swift's first biographers described
her as an ambitious coquette, a frivolous parvenue, a
Dean-eating harpy and a disillusioned drunkard. The
Victorian biographers and their immediate successors
gratefully accepted these descriptions of her and did
their best to show what a hard time Swift had trying to
fight her off and keep to the strait and narrow way. This
way was represented by Hester Johnson, on whose goodness all biographers have agreed: after eating her roast
beef like dragons they have run off and left poor Miss
Vanhomrigh with the bill.

In view of this it is refreshing to think that none of
the early biographers who were so rude about Miss Vanhomrigh had ever met her. All we know about her character is contained in Swift's letters to her and hers to
him: the rest belongs to that astonishing world of legend
and hearsay that has made both Hester Johnson and
Swift illegitimate Temples, engaged them in a secret
marriage, denied them that marriage because they were
uncle and niece, or brother and sister, and so on. As to
Miss Vanhomrigh, we do not know even what she
looked like, still less if she quarrelled with Swift over his
"marriage" to Miss Johnson and, dying drunken and
unforgiving, punished him by leaving half her money
to the metaphysician George Berkeley (then Dean of
Derry) and the other half to a young barrister, neither
of which legatees she had ever met in her life. But it is
curious that biographers who have made so much of
Swift's efforts to keep Miss Vanhomrigh at a distance
when she was alive should take it for granted that he
would expect to get her money when she was dead; even
the dullest among us know that legacies are not the

consequence of persistent disengagement. The matter is
the more curious because we find the same sort of rumour attaching to the death of Hester Johnson five years
later, when, we are told, a deathbed quarrel caused the
revising of Miss Johnson's will in favour of charity instead
of Swift. But if we are to guess at all in such matters,
should we not take Swift's usual behaviour into account?
We know that he was always afraid of gossip respecting
his relations with both women, particularly when he had
reached the rank of Dean and was living in a small,
prying world: does it seem likely that he would look to
these women for legacies that would confirm the tattle
of the town? Moreover, would not a desire for such
legacies be quite out of line with his characteristic feelings about such matters? Charitable causes, deserving
persons and honest relations (if such could be found)
were his preferences in the matter of wills, and it seems
not merely ungenerous but base not even to wonder if he
himself did not guide both the ladies in the making of
their wills. In leaving her small fortune to a Dublin
hospital, Miss Johnson only did what Swift himself was
to do. In leaving half hers to George Berkeley, Miss Vanhomrigh provided the philosopher with money that Swift
was trying hard to obtain for him elsewhere.

The matter is important not merely because it concerns money but because it concerns Swift. It has been
noted that when he was fond of someone he excused
their failings very readily, and this must be remembered
respecting his relations with Berkeley. That clergyman,
needless to say, was a metaphysician; Swift, needless to
say, detested metaphysics. But he was extremely fond of
Berkeley and, as Gibbon might put it, believed that the
uprightness of the divine excused the folly of the projector. He described *The Principles of Human Knowledge*
(1710) as "a very curious book", but he introduced its
author to court and London society, presenting him to
Lord Berkeley of Stratton with the words: "My lord,

here is a kinsman of your's whose acquaintance will confer more honour upon your lordship than your lordship's
acquaintance will confer upon him." He got Berkeley his
first official post, that of chaplain to the ambassador to
Sicily, Lord Peterborough, and continued forever after
to be his affectionate friend and helper. When Miss
Vanhomrigh died, leaving Berkeley £3,000, the philosopher thought it a "providential event", coming as it did
from one "to whom I was a perfect stranger". But that
the Providence behind the event may have been Swift
is suggested by the warmth of a letter he wrote on
Berkeley's behalf to Lord Carteret, the Lord-Lieutenant,
eight months after Miss Vanhomrigh's death, when her
affairs were still confused and her legacies unpaid.

Your Excellency will be frightened . . . for I am now to
mention his errand. He is an absolute philosopher, with
regard to money, titles, and power, and for three years past
has been struck with a notion of founding a University at
Bermudas. . . . He showed me a little tract which he designs
to publish [that is, *The Scheme for Converting the Savage
Americans to Christianity*], and there Your Excellency will
see his whole scheme of a life academico-philosophical . . . of
a college founded for Indian scholars and missionaries; where
he most exorbitantly proposes a whole hundred pounds a year
for himself, forty pounds for a fellow, and ten for a student.
His heart will break if his deanery be not taken from him,
and left to your Excellency's disposal. I discouraged him, by
the coldness of Courts and Ministers, who will interpret all
this as impossible, and a vision, but nothing will do; and
therefore I humbly entreat your Excellency, either to use such
persuasions as will keep one of the first men in this kingdom
for learning and virtue quiet at home, or assist him by your
credit, to compass his romantic design, which, however, is
very noble and generous, and directly proper for a great
person of your excellent education to encourage.

We do not understand Swift at all if we fail to understand how much he admired a clergyman who asked
nothing but to be shorn of the richest deanery in Ireland

and sent out with a pittance to preach the gospel in Bermuda. It was "romantic"; it was a "vision", and one may see that Swift had doubts about it. But we may consider, to say the least, that when Miss Vanhomrigh left money to this project, she was guided not by hatred of Swift but by amiable obedience to his advice. There is plenty of evidence to show Swift's fondness for Miss Vanhomrigh and Berkeley, but there is only rumour to suggest that the philosopher's legacy was the Parthian shot of a vindictive woman.

❋   ❋   ❋

Miss Vanhomrigh was a fairly early intruder into the long, platonic friendship of Swift and Hester Johnson. That friendship, which was built, as Swift tells us

>   Without one word of Cupid's darts,
>   Of killing eyes, or bleeding hearts

and

>   ne'er admitted Love a guest

was well established on a permanent footing in Ireland by the end of 1707, when Swift became first acquainted both with the Vanhomrigh family and Cupid's darts. Mrs. Vanhomrigh's London house was Swift's *pied à terre* during the years of his work with the Tory ministry, and we note as we read the *Journal to Stella* his increasing reluctance to mention his constant visits to the Vanhomrighs: he appears to be in the very common position of a man who is in something of a fix, conducting in one city a relationship that he hopes will not be known in the city in which he has another. Probably, he was not successful in this, lacking as he did the talents of a ship's captain or commercial traveller and being prominent enough in London to excite rumours that found their way to Dublin: we cannot be sure that Hester Johnson heard these tales and took offence, but the poem *In Sickness*, which stresses so insistently Swift's entire friendlessness at the time, can be read to suggest that something of this kind may have happened.

Esther, Mrs. Vanhomrigh's elder daughter, was not only intelligent enough to satisfy the headmaster in Swift but charming enough to carry the relationship far beyond that of teacher and pupil. Had she followed the rule of discretion that he was always urging on her, their intimacy would have remained limited; but Miss Vanhomrigh had both the skill and the courage to disobey Swift in pursuit of her inclinations and, as a result, to win his admiration without losing his respect. The disobediences for which he rebuked her became, in time, charming "surprises" that he looked back on happily: if she kept him in a constant fright, it was a faculty that made her the more attractive to him. When Swift settled into the deanery of St. Patrick's, Miss Vanhomrigh followed him almost immediately, and where formerly she had tried to sell her Irish property to ·support her in London, she now settled in Ireland, where she remained until her death in 1723, meeting Swift secretly and very frequently and corresponding with him when they were apart.

Not all their letters have survived, and it is the absence of correspondence in the last eight months of Miss Vanhomrigh's life that has been adduced as evidence of their having quarrelled horribly before she died. But it is just as likely that the letters are missing because Berkeley, the co-executor, found them to be the very opposite of quarrelsome and destroyed them to save his friend's reputation. A hard-hearted biographer with a caustic turn of mind could, indeed, play very plausibly with the hypothesis that the Dean having provided a legacy for the philosopher, the philosopher, in return, provided a bolt-hole for the Dean.

The surviving letters prove a very intimate relationship, which Swift manages to hide to a considerable extent and which Miss Vanhomrigh fails to hide at all.

The exact extent of the intimacy is not known and Swift's cousin, Deane, assured the world that any visits paid by Swift to Miss Vanhomrigh were only made with the object of finding out how she was coming along in her studies of the classics. But when a woman writes to a man: "We have had a vast deal of thunder and lightning; where do you think I wished to be then, and do you think that was the only time I wished so, since I saw you?" it would be wrong to insist that she was only wrapped up in books.

Esther Vanhomrigh was not merely in love with Swift; she worshipped him as if he were God, and she had the temerity to say so in plain writing, pointing out that while God was invisible and consequently hard to credit, Swift was entirely in evidence and impossible to doubt. It is no wonder that the Dean sprang this way and that in his efforts to disarm such flattering blasphemy, yet never succeeded either in modifying her tone or denying its charming effects. She has left us a priceless idea of what he looked like: "Sometimes you strike me with that prodigious awe, I tremble with fear; at other times a charming compassion shines through your countenance, which revives my soul": this is not lover's rhetoric, for Orrery—writing, by an odd coincidence, of the effect Swift's countenance had upon Miss Vanhomrigh—says: "DR. SWIFT had a natural severity of face, which even his smiles could scarce soften, or his utmost gaiety render placid and serene: but when that sternness of visage was encreased by rage, it is scarce possible to imagine looks, or features, that carried in them more terror and austerity". He sat among his Chapter, Orrery tells us, "like JUPITER in the Synod of the Gods", and as Jupiter he was seen, very properly, by his thunder-fearing nymph.

Swift never drops the decorum he imposed on his letters to her: he tries, it seems, to make the lavishness of his compliments make up for the paucity of passionate words. He thought her an incomparable letter writer—

which, indeed, she was, combining passion with style
and emotion with clarity: "If you write as you do", he
told her, when she had written to demand a visit, "I shall
come [to see you] the seldomer, on purpose to be pleased
with your letters, which I never look into without won-
dering how a brat who cannot read can possibly write
so well". She was, of course, a most diligent reader—
among other books, of *Gulliver's Travels*, parts of which
she was shown in manuscript five years before the world
saw them in print. Her conversation was of an equally
high order: "I never heard a single phrase escape your
lips that could have been expressed better". But what
impressed him as much as anything was precisely the
quality that made it impossible for her to be discreet—
her unfailing frankness and naturalness. And this is the
most interesting point of all respecting their relationship,
because it tells us so much about Swift. He might preach
about discretion, he might wake in the morning, as he
did once in London, muttering a dream-sentence: "I have
advised APRONIA to be careful, particularly about the
legs", but his heart was warmed by frankness and cooled
by prudence: if Berkeley rather than a cooler sort of
divine was his choice, Miss Vanhomrigh was similarly
preferred to APRONIA. Not only was she the only
representative in Ireland of the unconstricted world he
had known in England, she was also the model by which
he judged others of her sex. "I have never been able to
find any sort of defect in either your words or your
actions", he writes: "Coquetry, affection, prudery, are
imperfections unknown to you". Compared with her, he
insists, the other women he sees in Dublin are mere
"beasts in petticoats"—creatures of so wretched a sort
that he can scarcely believe them to be members of the
same sex and species as Miss Vanhomrigh.

It is not important for us to know if Miss Vanhomrigh
was in fact such an astonishing person. But it is very
important to note that the scorn of conventional women

that we find in *The Progress of Love* and the almost
bestial disgust that marks *The Progress of Beauty* are of
the same year (1719) as the letter quoted above: so, too,
is the like description of the naked ladies-in-waiting in
The Voyage to Brobdignag. In the first of the two poems
it is the discreet, sanctimonious prude that chooses to
elope with the brutish ostler; in the second it is a whore,
a veritable "beast in petticoats", that marks her real
foulness with surface paint and apparent beauty. We
who assume the existence of a middle state between the
perfection of Miss Vanhomrigh and the rottenness of
"Celia" must force ourselves to realize that such a middle
was fast ceasing to exist for Swift. From this time on it
was his expressed determination to laud selected human
beings while damning the mass of men as odious, and
though this act of will was often contradicted by his
personal behaviour, Swift upheld it on paper with fierce-
ness and stubbornness. Miss Vanhomrigh was present at
the inception of this violent point of view, and though
we are in no position to deny Swift's sincerity in describing her as a woman apart from the rest, we may see this
appraisal as an illustration of how he had resolved to
think. It is at this point in his life that mankind in general
become Yahoos and are made to stand in entire contrast
to the perfection of horses: one might even suggest that
Miss Vanhomrigh's perfections are to some extent part
of a literary exercise—indeed, that she becomes a willing
student and living example of literary creation. Middleton Murry has tried to prove what amounts to the opposite of this: he is confident that the Yahoos are Swift's
response to Miss Vanhomrigh's death in 1723: her death,
in Murry's view, obliged Swift to recognize how badly
he had treated both her and Hester Johnson in refusing
them a normal, sexual relationship: rather than admit
this, he trounced them as beasts, dwelling specially on
the nasty, copulative propensities of the she-Yahoo.

To this thesis there are two replies: the first, that Book

IV of *Gulliver's Travels* concerns the species as a whole
and condemns he-Yahoos as much as shes; the second,
that Miss Vanhomrigh seems to have had the pleasure of
reading Book IV at least one year before she died. Far
from being personally offended by its she-Yahoos, she
related them promptly to the ladies of her own circle,
describing herself among them in a letter to Swift of
1722 in much the same words as he had used to describe
Gulliver among the Yahoos of his fiction. Miss Vanhomrigh's tone is a little smug, but this is to be expected
from an adoring pupil who has been accorded pre-
publication privileges by Jupiter.

One examines this matter thoroughly in order to suggest that the Yahoos formed a broad state of mind in
Swift at this time, rather than a repressed and narrow
preoccupation with his sexual deficiencies: they are a
retort to his awful fall and his friends' punishments rather
than an angry denial of personal guilt. The Yahoos
belong to the reviving self of 1719 to 1721: to this re-
creation of vigour Miss Vanhomrigh is more midwife
than bane. Dying, at only thirty-four, of a consumption
caught from her younger sister, whom she nursed to the
end, she is one of the few hymns of glory that Swift sang
in these years, and belongs to that small company of
individuals whom Swift dissociated entirely from the
remainder of mankind. These exceptions to the general
rule are not merely "great" men such as the fallen Harley
and the patriotic Archbishop King, nor are they only
"great" ladies such as the wives of Ormond and St. John.
They include his servant Alexander McGee, one of that
most detested breed of Scots, whose name Swift insisted
on changing to Saunders. We may still see today at St.
Patrick's the inscribed monument that the Dean set up
in memory of that unique Scot, and as we read the
tribute to that "best and most devoted of servants" we
may read, in effect, the will that dictated a dividing of
humanity into a chosen few and a contemptible bulk.

For, outside this small company, the Yahoos begin. A fixed decision has been made to see the world in these extreme terms: whether the material involved is fact or fiction, it is dealt with by a single state of mind. The joker in the pack, as is always the case with Swift, is that this remorseless outlook is impossible to maintain: the will decrees it, but the man, being more than will alone, is open to feelings that the decree is supposed to exclude. St. John is a most useful man in helping us to understand this, because he knows Swift very well and is never afraid to laugh at him for pretending to be other than he actually is. When Swift declares that the maxim of self-interest laid down by Rochefoucauld has always been his own guide—"I found my whole character in [Rochefoucauld]", he insists—St. John only laughs. When Swift expresses his cold disdain for mankind at large, St. John merely observes that in that case he has no business stirring up the Irish mob to fight for their liberties. Of course, St. John is quite right, and Swift's heated efforts to prove himself the coldest of cold fish provide a wonderfully comic part of their correspondence. But this conflict between what a man wills himself to be and what he really is can be comic only for so long: if persisted in, it is sure to become tragic. The older Swift becomes, the more wildly he insists upon his indifference to humanity, and the more he insists upon it, the more he displays his real distress and outrage. His "true" character becomes harder and harder to read because he is forever engaged in turning it into a beastly caricature, so that it is very difficult to know with whom one is dealing at any given moment: there is the Swift one knows, and there is a Swift who is not only being invented but claiming passionately that he has always been the real Swift. His friends rejected this claimant, and so do we; but we must be extremely careful not to deny that the invented image became the truer one in the end. When the young Swift read Hobbes's opinion that self-interest was the prime motive in all men he merely smiled and agreed—adding, however, that those who pleased themselves by doing good to others made better citizens than those who obtained their pleasure by being cruel. But when the elderly Swift found Hobbes's opinion repeated exactly by La Rochefoucauld he refused to affix to the repetition the rider he had nailed to the original: on the contrary, he swallowed Rochefoucauld's maxim whole with fierce satisfaction. It suited his book to do so; it suited the new character he was imposing upon himself: "This", he seems to say, "is how I mean to see the world and how I mean the world to see me". His strength of will was so great that he was able, at least, to act the part he had chosen for himself with considerable success and to hand down to legend the awful portrait of "The Dean" that has almost effaced the lineaments of "The Doctor". But it is the biographer's duty not to regard "The Dean" as a mere fiction imposed on an underlying reality: both "Doctor" and "Dean" come from the same stable.

*　　*　　*

Gulliver's Travels represents a magnificent triumph of the will and state of mind that have been described above. It begins with the will-power only partly roused and being employed with extreme grace, wit and subtlety; it ends with the will at its most vehement and monstrous, reflecting in this development the author's own march from his old self to his new one. It does not give the impression of having been planned as it stands from the start; on the contrary, it suggests that each part inspired its successor, and that the appetite grew with the feeding—a hunger for greater intensity and more powerful amplification being felt more and more strongly as the work proceeded. A great deal has been written about its originating in the ideas and table-talk of Swift and his London friends, but without questioning the correctness of this ascription, must we not also allow *Robinson*

Crusoe, which appeared in 1719, some of the honour of having set it going? We cannot do so with any firmness, unfortunately, but we can certainly use the one book as a point of departure for the other; for the two, seen side by side, form a wonderful pair, representing two sorts of writing, two entirely disparate views of fiction and two superbly opposed authors. To describe *Gulliver's Travels* as Swift's deliberate retort to *Robinson Crusoe* would be unwarranted, but if we amuse ourselves by considering it as such, the result is as informative as it is entertaining. Moreover, we never see Swift more clearly than in relation to Defoe: each demands the presence of the other, in the sense that each side demands the presence of the other if we are to understand a battle, a Parliamentary conflict, a divided nation.

Defoe embodies everything that Swift hates: he is the other half of England that Swift struggled all his life to suppress or ignore and by which he was defeated and driven into isolation. Defoe, with his brickworks and bankruptcies, is the rising small business man whom Swift saw very correctly as the man who would unseat his timocracy of landed gentlemen and substitute an economy of stocks and shares for one of estate and title. He is the Roundhead Dissenter to whom the Whigs run as an ally in their fight with the Tories of the Established Church—and, by turning to him, change what was formerly a private quarrel between Anglican landlords into a lasting division between regicide Puritan merchants and honourable county squires. Swift is the gentleman-author whose chosen home is society and the dignified sphere of the well-educated and well-born; Defoe is the born gander of Grub Street, the father of all that is noisiest and freest in modern journalism. Defoe is liberty in the form in which Swift detested it most: he is the rogue whom Swift loved best to "swinge", and his life is a constant, rapscallionly muddle, bursting with excitements and devoid of all dignity. Where Swift goes in danger of the Tower, Defoe's natural punishment is the pillory: the higher place is reserved for the treasonable gentleman, the lower for the provocative hack. The two men have only three things in common: the first is that they both took service under Harley, Swift as unpaid propagandist and Defoe as paid informer; the second is that they were both passionately in favour of the educating of women; and the third is that both were capable of satire. We expect satire from a Tory like Swift, but we are surprised and interested to find it in an enthusiastic Whig. Yet Defoe's *The Shortest Way with the Dissenters*, the satirical essay for which he was put in the pillory, anticipates exactly in tone and tendency Swift's *Modest Proposal* for dealing with surplus Irishmen: the only real difference between the two essays is that Defoe's makes its plea for the mutilating of Dissenters in rather a blunt way, whereas Swift's plea for eating babies is made with the refinement and gentility that we expect from a clergyman of the better class.

Of the two Defoe is by far the more sympathetic and agreeable man and fits most happily today into the excessively unaustere society that composes our democracy. He is the beginning of the social struggle of which we are the end, and he presses forward into modern times proportionately as Swift fights backwards into the time behind him. When we hold each man's masterpiece in our hands we hold the halves of one apple—the apple of discord that, in its wholeness, represents the England of the early eighteenth century.

Robinson Crusoe has been called aptly "the primary textbook of capitalism"—and who can resist the amusement of reading it as such? What author ever built such a warehouse or drew up a more satisfying inventory? Every page is a merchant's catalogue of hardware, woollens, leather goods and crockery, and from the fields outside the warehouse come the baaing of the good tradesman's flocks and the ripple of the breeze through his stalks of corn. All these goods, together with a snug house fenced and barricaded interminably against burglars, are available to the forceful capitalist, who, by diligent sowing of a little seed, builds his frugal investments into interest-bearing property. And how excitedly we labour with Crusoe, first for mere self-survival, later for a higher rate of interest and greater abundance of possessions! How we share his horrified terror when that most magical of all moments in fiction, the footprint in the sand, tells us brutally that some barbarous intruder threatens not only life but property! And how thankful we are to know that our heroic investor does not stand alone—that his marvels of free enterprise are noted and sanctioned by God Himself! For, certainly, there never was a book in which God's hand was busier—helping in the factory, making sound economical suggestions, keeping an eye on things generally and asking nothing in return but prayers—heart-felt prayers, of course; but who would *not* pray heartily to such a generous Father? No Puritan but Bunyan ever wrote a happier book; no merchant ever looked upon his gains and declared with greater self-satisfaction that the earth was the Lord's and the glory thereof.

At the time *Robinson Crusoe* appeared Swift was reading all the travel books he could find: they were all trash but a perfect antidote to the spleen, he assured Miss Vanhomrigh. Merely to imagine him reading *Robinson Crusoe* is enough to make one laugh, for it is pleasing to picture his contemptuous response to Defoe's unceasing power to declare, in all imaginable matters, his faith in all that Swift despised. Each author, to begin with, sets out upon his "Travels" with the intention of discovering only that which he already knows and erecting in a strange land that which he knows to have been built at home. Defoe turns a primitive island into a commercial enterprise: the only enemy to this sort of civilization is the naked savage—the terrifying cannibal whose primitive

appetites threaten disaster to the God-fearing business-
man. But Swift's islands are never menaced by barbarism:
on the contrary, the only atrocities he finds are those of
civilized, cultured persons who have degenerated grossly
from the happier, natural state of man and have espoused
reason only in order that "the corruption of that faculty
might be worse than brutality itself". Where Defoe looks
with horror at the naked footprint, Swift looks with equal
horror at the imprint of the court-shoe, and Gulliver,
even after being wounded by savages, would still prefer
"to trust myself among those barbarians, than live with
European Yahoos". The Dissenting merchant and re-
former never doubts that trade and colonization confer
civilized benefits upon savage people: it is the Tory
churchman who argues, with the modern radical, that
colonists are no better than an "execrable crew of butch-
ers" enjoying "a free license . . . to all acts of inhumanity
and lust".

Man himself, as he walks the world, drives the two
authors to opposite poles. Defoe will have no truck with
the naked body; his excitements come from the fabri-
cating of its garments out of the available raw materials
and from its foodstuffs and implements. But the High
Church Dean despises "the subject of . . . diet, wherewith
other travellers fill their books", and where Defoe asks
that we admire the fur hat and skin-breeches, Swift keeps
pulling off these contemptible disguises and pressing our
eyes and noses to the hairy warts and stenches of the flesh
below. The Puritan is far too respectable even to mention
the functions of the body, but the Dean's book abounds
in hogsheads of urine and the voiding of excrement. This
is why *Robinson Crusoe* is an essentially materialistic
book and yet a wholly unphysical one, whereas *Gulliver's
Travels* is only occasionally materialistic and always
passionately physical.

The numerous other "opposites" in the two books are
all very engaging and highly characteristic of their re-

spective authors. Crusoe is a simple man of Defoe's own class; Gulliver, like Sir William Temple, is a graduate of Emmanuel College, Cambridge. Unlike Defoe's God, the Dean's is much too detached and Olympian to be involved in Gulliver's absurd affairs—and Gulliver himself is much too much an average gentleman to waste a moment in prayer. The Dissenter, once he has built himself a small realm abroad, delights in allowing "liberty of conscience throughout my dominions"; the Dean, however, does not lose the opportunity of requiring the monarch of Brobdignag to assert that "a man may be allowed to keep poisons in his closet, but not to vend them about for cordials".

But the most entertaining contrast between the books, from a literary point of view, is in each author's declared intention. *Robinson Crusoe* is the work of a journalist; it is essentially what we would call a "documentary", or a blunt unpolished recital of the plain facts—yet it is of this documentary that Defoe says: "My story is a whole collection of wonders". *Gulliver's Travels*, on the other hand, *is* a whole collection of wonders—as much an imaginary creation as *Crusoe* is not and, for the most part, most admirably "turned" and polished. Yet Swift declares of it: "I could perhaps, like others, have astonished thee with strange, improbable tales; but I rather chose to relate plain matter of fact, in the simplest manner and style. . . ." Thus does each author indulge the perfectly excusable pretence that suits his book, the journalist seeking to elevate his facts into fancy, the wit to resolve pure fantasy into facts.

Robinson Crusoe, one may say, never gets off the ground at all: it is rarely touched by the imagination and asks nothing of the intellect. But *Gulliver's Travels* is a work of pure intellect, an act of unceasing invention. Defoe, patiently assembling material facts, needs forty pages of preliminaries to wreck his hero on a desert island; Swift, anxious to leave the factual world behind,

carries Gulliver to Lilliput in little more than a page.
Defoe, having retailed one fact, merely goes on to retail
the next fact; but the chief purpose served by a fact in
Swift is to be a spring-board into fantasy. And nothing
about *Gulliver's Travels* is more interesting than to study
the way in which this fantasy is anchored—to see why,
even at its most fantastic moments, it does not lose its
ties with the earth. To see how Swift does this, is to see
what satire must always do if its angry fantasies are to
be brought safely home.

* * *

Napoleon, discussing at St. Helena the innovations of
the French Revolution, declared himself entirely in
favour of the change made by the revolutionary intellectuals to the Metric System of weights and measures.
But he pointed out that the mathematicians who arranged
this change made a typical academic mistake: by throw-
ing away the old *terms*, they turned weights and measures into inhuman abstractions. The man who works with
a terminology of *hands*, *feet* and *ells* in effect bases all
his calculations on the parts of his body: even when he
speaks in terms of *poles* and *chains*, he is still speaking
of what he regards as extensions of his own arms. But
once he must calculate in *ares* and *metres*, he must lose
his sense of physical conjunction with the world, and the
loss of this sensuous tie, Napoleon believed, was precisely the sort of loss that always should be avoided in
the modernising of ancient systems.

In this spasm of light from a dying star we see clearly
one of the great strengths of *Gulliver's Travels*—the
anchoring of the high-flying mind to the physical body.
This is not the book of an abstract "projector" calculating
in a world apart; it is a book in which man *is* the measure
of all things. We find this first, of course, in the simple
matter of relative sizes in Lilliput and Brobdignag, but
it is the actual estimating of these proportions—the terms

in which they are assessed—that is so unabstract and gives the book its fleshy solidity. Like Defoe, Swift will often tell us how small or large a thing was by giving its linear measurement; but, unlike Defoe, he prefers to lay a human limb alongside it, to make his comparison, and to press our eyes, noses and ears into the service of his imaginings. In the huge magnifications of Brobdignag, the purring of a cat is not described in mere adjectival sonorities; instead, it is "like that of a dozen stocking-weavers at work". A gigantic infant's cry is "a squall that you might have heard from London Bridge to Chelsea"; and twenty wasps, "as large as partridges", sweep in at the window "humming louder than the drone of as many bagpipes". The Brobdignagian queen can "craunch the wing of a lark, bones and all, between her teeth, although it were nine times as large as that of a full-grown turkey", and her table knives are "twice as long as a scythe". Each fly is of the greatness of "a Dunstable lark" and, as it walks, demonstrates its essential monstrousness to the eye of the tiny observer by leaving behind it a loathsome trail of excrement, spawn and "viscous matter". One paring from the Queen's thumbnail serves for the back of a horn comb, bladed with "stumps of the King's beard"; the corn on the toe of a royal maid-of-honour is of "about the bigness of a Kentish pippin"; sliced from its owner and carried home to England, it can be "hollowed into a cup, and set in silver". Waves of overpowering stench and scent are emitted by the naked bodies of those royal maids, and each charming mole that spots the skin stands "broad as a trencher, and hairs hanging from it thicker than packthreads". The thump on the scaffold floor of a murderer's decapitated head is such as to shake the ground for "at least half an English mile", while—most astonishing simile of all—the "veins and arteries [of the trunk] spouted up such a prodigious quantity of blood, and so high in the air, that the great *jet d'eau* at Versailles was not equal for the time it lasted". Reversed in their proportions to fit the world of Lilliput, the similes are more charming than gross, but they always retain their intense, familiar quality—tiny men ploughing through Gulliver's snuff-box "up to the mid-leg in a sort of dust" and sneezing dreadfully as they go; examining letters and diaries in which every character is "almost half as large as the palm of our hands"; discovering a pocket-watch, "which the emperor was very curious to see, and commanded two of his tallest yeoman of the guards to bear it on a pole upon their shoulders, as draymen in England do a barrel of ale". "I have been much pleased", says Gulliver, "with a cook pulling a lark, which was not so large as a common fly; and a young girl threading an invisible needle with invisible silk".

This intense proximity, this use of commonplaces to ground the imagination, has a curious effect. It is not noticed by the reader when he finds it pleasing: he merely smiles at the image without inquiring into the techniques that have made him smile. But when the simile is gross—when excrement and hairy moles replace invisible needles and snuff—he not only sees the technique but begins to wonder what sort of man the author was. Yet it should be plain that the same method is being used throughout and that there is a grand unity of treatment that covers in one way the nicest and nastiest things. For every grossness in Swift there is a corresponding delicacy—a point nicely made by Pope in his well-known lines on Swift. But whichever course, fine or gross, he chooses to take, an intensely personal intimacy lies at the core of it. The grand flights of his imagination are made plausible only by the point from which they take their departure, and this point is always the living human being and his familiar belongings, sensations and habits. Nor is there any limit to the use of this admirable art; it can be applied not only to the coarsest and most delicate things but also to the occasions when genius displays itself by listing details in the simplest way and then turning them, without the least change of expression, to irresistibly human account:

"... Their manner of writing is very peculiar, being neither from the left to the right, like the Europeans; nor from the right to the left, like the Arabians; nor from up to down, like the Chinese; but aslant, from one corner of the paper to the other, like ladies in England."

The life we share with Robinson Crusoe has no place for such extraordinary felicities. It is, in the friendliest sense of the words, merely a life of gain, technical security, adventure and everyday ingenuity; it provides neither insight into human behaviour nor interest in human thought. *Gulliver's Travels* begins where *Robinson Crusoe* ends; it enquires and reflects where the other rests content to act and possess. We see Crusoe naked only when he is afraid, but we see Gulliver in all his human weaknesses—in his fear, his vanity, his pride, his shame, his shivering little skin. Neither Gulliver nor Crusoe is of much interest as a principal character, but each is uninteresting for a different reason—Crusoe because his material possessions loom larger than he does, Gulliver because his story would have no solid centre if he himself were made as dramatically extraordinary as the situations and persons he meets: in this respect we may compare him to the plain Martin in *A Tale of a Tub*. We ask that Gulliver be a bigger man only for one reason—we cannot forgive him for surrendering to the Houyhnhnms and recognising in himself and us the beastly image of a Yahoo. And we do not forgive him for this because we shall never forgive Swift for it.

A good way to examine this matter is to compare good-humouredly the conclusions of *Robinson Crusoe* and *Gulliver's Travels*. In both books, the hero is carried safe back to Europe by a kindly ship's captain, a Portuguese in Gulliver's case, an Englishman in Crusoe's. We

know the revulsion that the return to the world excites
in Gulliver—how he shrinks from the touch of his own
wife and children, how repugnant he finds the stench
and character of the Yahoo. But we should remember,
too, how different the world seems to Defoe's returning
castaway. Crusoe finds that the world is good—indeed,
that it is overflowing with probity and justice. The
twenty-eight years of his absence have been devoted by
his honest partners to the preservation and increase of
his investments, and the totting up of the grand total,
with the occasional pause for an *Ave Maria*, forms a most
suitable conclusion to this best of mercantile books.
Twelve hundred chests of sugar, 800 rolls of tobacco,
thousands of golden Portuguese moidores, large Brazilian
plantations worked assiduously by black slaves: it all
amounts to "above £5,000 sterling" and a South Ameri-
can estate of "above £1,000 a year". And when we hear
the chink of those moidores, do we not exclaim with
Crusoe: "It is impossible to express the flutterings of my
very heart when I looked over these letters and especially
when I found all my wealth about me"? Do we not agree
most heartily with him that "the latter end of Job was
better than the beginning"? And are we at all surprised
to find Job in that *galère*?

This is the happy end we all want—honest men, a
banker-God, and accumulated interest. Defoe never
denied it even to the worst of us: once Moll Flanders
stopped being a whore and a thief and invested in probity and God, her income rose in due proportion with her
piety, cementing the delights of capital to the forgiveness of sins. And because we feel that things *should* turn
out like this in a novel—that money is what Job is being
so patient about; that money is what Swift loses when
Miss Vanhomrigh dies—we are profoundly offended when
Gulliver shrinks from touching us, and his author, peeling
us down to mere skin and claws, wipes us from his sight
as stinking Yahoos. His terrible insult has survived two

centuries unimpaired: it hurts us today even more than it hurt its first readers. Many, indeed, protest that no author who really believed in God could find it in his heart to condemn us so unkindly; others, more expert in the study of Swift, have turned the insult by tracing it to a psychological deformation in the author. All of which has one very amusing result—that we regard *Robinson Crusoe*, which is a documentary, as an acceptable piece of fiction, but dismiss *Gulliver's Travels*, which is a pure fiction, as a libellous piece of documentary. Yet this absurd conclusion suits both authors admirably, for Defoe, as has been noted, pretended to be a teller of wonders, while Swift pretended to be a reporter of facts. The journalist set out to please his public; the Dean intended to roast it. Both authors succeeded admirably in their intentions, and both are read still in the spirit in which they wrote. Both would be overjoyed to know it.

＊　　＊　　＊

When we consider the closing years of Swift's life, we wonder at the vehemence and indignation which accompanied them. For we note what an extremely full life it was—always active, always marked by triumphant battles, always glowing with a popularity amounting to idolatry. We recognize that we are dealing with an outlaw, but the deanery which constitutes the outlaw's cave seems to us as proud and powerful a cave as any outlaw could ask for—a veritable kingdom-in-small, protected and worshipped by the Dublin mob and constituting such a fortress that the arrest of its commander would require, as Walpole is said to have been warned, an expeditionary force of twenty thousand soldiers. More than two hundred years after the event, we thrill to Orrery's account of the response that Swift received when, under the alias of "M. B. Drapier", he wrote the famous open letter summoning "the whole people of Ireland" to oppose the degrading of their kingdom to the state of a subject colony:

At the sound of the DRAPIER'S trumpet, a spirit arose among the people, that, in the eastern phrase, was *like unto a trumpet in the day of the whirlwind.* . . . The Papist, the Fanatic, the Tory, the Whig, all listed themselves volunteers under the banner of M. B. DRAPIER . . . the name of AUGUSTUS was not bestowed upon OCTAVIUS CAESAR with more universal approbation, than the name of THE DRAPIER was bestowed upon THE DEAN. He . . . became the idol of the people of *Ireland* to a degree of devotion, that in the most superstitious country scarce any idol ever obtained. . . . His effigies were painted in every street in *Dublin.* Acclamations and vows for his prosperity attended his footsteps wherever he passed. He was consulted in all Points relating to domestic policy in general, and to the trade of Ireland in particular. . . . In this state of power, and popular love and admiration, he remained till he lost his senses. . . .

So affecting is the spirit of this, and so impressive the energetic character of its patriot leader, that we feel for a moment that the Deanery of St. Patrick's was the turbulent centre of the whole universe, and Hanoverian England merely a Lilliput on the outskirts of the Drapier-Dean's domain. Alas! this is only the optical delusion of biography, which, once profoundly attached to its hero, is happy to turn the planet on his figure. To see Swift as he was, and as he saw himself, we must leave him and his impassioned idolaters and go to England; and when we do this, the proportions are so reversed that his distress becomes understandable immediately. The England of Walpole and the first two Georges went about its business with absolute disregard for the outlawed Dean; at most, he was a nuisance, at least, a political nonentity. If his many friends in the Tory Opposition in England were of slight importance, his own, isolated in Dublin, was strictly local, and one may read memoirs of the times and find hardly a mention of his name. As a man of letters, he grew into a giant; as a "lion", his appearance could always command attention; but as a politician and a courtier he had ceased to exist.

It is in this neglected state that we must see his situation and understand his increasing belligerence. The poems in which he describes how little notice will be taken of his death are not exercises in sarcasm but sardonic statements of fact; the numerous letters in which he laments furiously his deprived and lonely state are not exaggerated in their vehemence. To us the patriotic fate to which he was destined in Ireland seems infinitely grander than any role he might have played at the court of George II; indeed, we may feel thankful that he was spared the degradation of such an association. For, if the world, as Swift saw it, had declined horribly from the time of Charles I to Queen Anne, with what words can one express the drop that was the Hanoverians? Yet the truth is that Gulliver's revulsion from Yahoos and his tendency to fall into a swoon on finding himself among them was not shared by his author. Swift was no William Tell or Andreas Hofer; he loved courts; he loved, as he says in the *Journal*, to attend the drawing-rooms and watch the world go by. Pope might write lightly: "Courts I see not, courtiers I know not, Kings I adore not, Queens I compliment not", but Swift, in the same boat, could never go on to say: "I despise the world yet . . . and the Court more than all the rest of the world". He hankered after court life and ministerial recognition, but the reconciliation he desired had to be of the sort he was used to—the great must come to him, not he to the great. If Queen Caroline wished to see him, she must make advances to him like other great ladies—and he was proud to declare that she did so no less than nine times before he would respond to her summons. Moreover, he must be invited by her because his merits commanded an invitation and because he had wise advice to give her, not merely because "she had a curiosity to see a wild Dean from Ireland". To put it shortly, in coming to Court, Swift would confer an honour upon the Court, and though we agree heartily that this could not fail to be true, we see also that it could never happen, as there never was a court prepared to reconcile itself with an outlawed subject on terms as haughty as that. Nor was there ever a government which would patch up a quarrel with a dangerous exile by inviting him home and giving him preferment—in return for obeying his dictates and having to suffer him the fullest liberty to speak and write as he chose. What Swift asked of England was the power he had seized in Ireland: refused this, he preferred exile, saying: "I would rather be a freeman among slaves, than a slave among freemen". But it angered him intensely to be obliged to make this choice, and the older he became, the more indignantly he spoke of those who had rejected his terms and obliged him to maintain his dignity by staying in exile. Swift, as Irish patriot, has been written about somewhat sarcastically: revenge for personal humiliation has been suggested as the true reason for his espousal of the Irish cause. But what has not been said so clearly is that Swift himself insisted on preferring this very charge against himself. Far from denying the personal motive, he insisted triumphantly upon it. "I will kill that louse or flea which bites me, though I get no honour by it", he assured Sheridan; and to Lord Bathhurst, in 1730, he was explicit, saying: "If any kingdom was ever in a right situation of breeding poets, it is this, whither you and your crew unpardonably sent me sixteen years ago, and where I have been ever since, studying as well as preaching revenge, malise, envy and hatred, and all un-charitableness". Yet in the following sentence itself he continues: "And I desire, by Grace, Lady Bathurst may not be angry, for I do assure her upon the word of a Dean that it is all the pure uncorrupt fruit of a true public spirit". And so the strain continues in letter after letter, with the personal motive forever entwining itself with the spirit of the public good, and each receiving in its turn an equally emphatic stress. Thus we feel at one moment the fury of the man "left to die, like a poisoned rat in a hole", and at the next the same fury poured out in an intense description of the public misery; for example, the condition of Tipperary:

. . . The whole kingdom, a bare face of nature, without houses or plantations; filthy cabins, miserable, tattered, half-starved creatures, scarce in human shape; one insolent ignorant oppressive squire to be found in twenty miles riding; a parish church only to be found in a summer day's journey, in comparison of which, an English farmer's barn is a cathedral; a bog of fifteen miles round; every meadow a slough, and every hill a mixture of rock, heath, and marsh; and every male and female, from the farmer, inclusive to the day-labourer, infallibly a thief, and consequently a beggar, which in this island are terms convertible. . . . There is not an acre of land in Ireland turned half to its advantage, yet it is better improved than the people; and all these evils are effects of English tyranny, so your sons and grandchildren will find it to their sorrow. . . .

Many have been perplexed by what they have felt to be the problem of deciding between the personal revenger and the public defender. Yeats, in a famous essay, tried to remove the problem by suggesting that Swift's patriotism *could* not be explained, psychologically or otherwise; it must be seen, he said, as a sort of inexplicable phenomenon thrown up by the convulsions of a suffering nation. But there is no need to call upon such a mysterious explanation. When a great man, driven into exile in the prime of his life, swearing revenge and full of fight, finds in that exile thousands of others in a condition far more lamentable than his own, what is more natural than that there should be an union of forces in which what is personal becomes scarcely separable from what is public? The ignominy that Swift suffered came, in his opinion, from the same source as the ignominy that Ireland suffered; and with the passing years, both Swift and Ireland suffered that same ignominy more than ever: their conditions always became worse, never better. The very grandeur of Swift's Irish years depends not only on this striking coincidence of personal and public miseries, but on the fact that Swift never fought the first without regard for the second. And was this mixture not characteristic of him all his life? Can we hope ever to understand him even in the most superficial way if we do not resign ourselves to the fact that the chief peculiarity of his personality was that it was a meeting-place for such diversities? The "mazy turnings of his character" made Orrery say that "of all mankind, SWIFT perhaps had the greatest contrasts in his temper", reminding his biographer of the "Manichean superstition quoted by Plutarch: 'That we are subject to the influence of two principles, or deities, who are in constant opposition to each other. . . .' To list but a few of these "oppositions", we have a bachelor who cannot live without women; a despot with a passion for liberty; a sour divine who plays like a child; an author who stakes his whole career on his wit but rarely admits that he is an author at all; a tight-fisted man who spends liberally on charity; a creature so humane as to feel infinite distress for the insane but describes the bestowing of his fortune on them as "a satiric touch". The numerous pseudonyms under which Swift wrote are themselves the character that he loved to conceal—a character that obtained infinite pleasure from riddles and disguises and found the most obstinate satisfaction in making his savagery look virtuous and his unselfishness look unkind. And once we accept this eccentric obstinacy, we have no need to speak of characteristic "oppositions". These are, rather, the elements of a characteristic unity.

One may still, however, ask *why* a man whose straight-

forwardness and honesty were so valued by his friends
went to such lengths to propound himself as a sort of
riddle. The answer appears to be not one answer but
many answers, some of which are very simple to understand. That he should, for instance, persist in calling himself a Whig, particularly at moments when he was most
Tory, was merely his stubborn way of insisting that he
maintained the principles with which the Whigs had
started; broadly speaking, this was true. That he took
pride in being a clergyman but saw no reason why he
should "act" the part was his very proper way of insisting
that clergymen be accepted as a normal element in society rather than as embarrassing freaks. Of the combination in him of a headmasterly passion for discipline and a
childish delight in the trivial frivolities of puns and word-
games, one need only say that it is a common combination in schoolmasters, who hew severely to the line in
important matters and depart from it almost too readily
in insignificant ones: it is their way of playing. We also
know very well the sort of men who dislike admitting
that they are soft-hearted and disguise their frequent
kindnesses as acts of selfishness; nor are we strangers to
those who are parsimonious in some matters and generous in others: this mixture is common to all of us. But
as to the numerous other "opposites" in Swift, they can
be understood, as a rule, only in the light of his declared
ambition, his pride, and his insistence that his merits be
discovered by others rather than vaunted by himself.
Pride is more satisfied when the author of a work refuses
to declare himself and must be detected as the author.by
virtue of his inimitable style. It is prouder to deny one's
merits than to boast them, and prouder to oblige states-
men and ladies to make "advances" than it is to advance
oneself. Moreover, a man's dignity is better secured by
such methods—and there can be no doubt that Swift's
sense of personal dignity was quite enormous. He was
always conscious of having made his way in the world

without credentials of birth or fortune, and his fear of being snubbed or affronted did not encourage him ever to risk his dignity by pushing his claims either as a man or an author.

It may seem absurd to us that the publishing of *Gulliver's Travels* should have been arranged by an invented character named "Richard Sympson"—and hailed as Jonathan Swift's the very moment it appeared: whom did Swift pretend he was hoaxing? But such acts were not mere games to Swift, much as he loved games. He required the public, too, to make its advances to him; moreover, it is unlikely that he ever lost the feeling of self-doubt that disturbs every good writer. In pseudonyms and anonymity he provided himself with a back door: if his merits were rejected and his dignity snubbed, he had a way out. It is when Swift is really cornered— when his fears for his dignity have led him to a rashness from which he cannot escape—that he vents his humiliation in angry spite. And where there is so much fear of offence to dignity, there is almost bound to be a constant suspicion of such an offence and even a frequent detection of it where it does not exist. This is why, as Swift grows older, so much of his life reads like a gloss on two items from his *Thoughts on Various Subjects*:

Dignity and Station, or great Riches, are in some Sort necessary to old Men, in order to keep the younger at a Distance, who are otherwise too apt to insult them upon the Score of their Age.

Imaginary Evils soon become real ones, by indulging our Reflections on them; as he, who, in a melancholy Fancy, seeth something like a Face on the Wall or the Wainscot, can, by two or three Touches with a leaden Pencil, make it look visible and agreeing with what he fancied.

＊ ＊ ＊

The first face to receive the touch of this "leaden Pencil" was that of the lady who was Swift's chief hope of returning into favor with the Court. Mrs. Howard had been George II's mistress for many years, but by the time the King came to the throne he was tired of her and plagued to death by her efforts to recommend the sort of people he most disliked; for he took pride in the fact that where other men loved literature until late in life, he himself had seen through its pretensions when he was still a small boy. When poor Mrs. Howard failed utterly to bring Swift into favour with this corpus of headstrong puerility, Swift was filled with evil imaginings of her, particularly as he had followed her advice and paid his respects to the new king at the moment that she had chosen as the most propitious. When it proved to be nothing of the sort Mrs. Howard became Swift's chief aversion on a double count: first, she had played the courtier and told him lies; second, by causing him to believe her lies and act on them, she had brought on him the huge humiliation of a royal snub. But in a footnote to one of his poems, we find mention of a third count, which outweighs the others in importance. Mrs. Howard's good offices, we find, were expected to bring Swift's exile to an end and procure him "a settlement in England". We can understand his hatred of her only if we understand that he made her responsible for the destruction of his last hope of returning to England: this, perhaps, was the worst blow he ever received and one from which he was never able to recover.

The poor lady protested her innocence in some of the kindest and humblest letters that Swift ever received: in his hard, cold retorts we see the ardent believer in friendship wilfully destroying one of the best friendships of his life. Nor does the destruction of old friendship stop with Mrs. Howard, for when an even greater friend of Swift's, Lady Elizabeth Germaine, daughter of his old patron the Earl of Berkeley, defended Mrs. Howard with infinite gentleness and the fullest regard for Swift's dignity, she too fell under suspicion and was eventually dismissed for ever from his heart. To read this dreadful exchange of letters is to see Swift at his worst and his friends at their best: Pope himself, braving Swift's anger in defence of Mrs. Howard, shines momentarily with a knightly lustre.

But it is the women that answer Swift best, and in doing so show not only how fond they were of him but how far his hopelessness had pushed him beyond appeals to reason, kindness and common sense. Swift's letters are inimitably good—more natural and straightforward than Pope's, more heart-felt and intimate than St. John's—but we must accustom ourselves in this period to finding their ardour tainted with hysterical querulousness and their honesty with petty suspiciousness and unreasonable indignation: these small savageries of expression are the lesser outbursts of a harrowing disappointment. To this are added the outcries of a man inflamed by grievances, public as well as private, and tortured by a head roaring and spinning with the worsening disease of his ears.* The man who was a stranger to the spleen is being slowly conquered by it and, with every year, coming nearer to the age when past losses and disappointments mean far more than future hopes. His rigidity and harshness

* "Ménière's Syndrome", first diagnosed in 1861 and known also as aural vertigo and labyrinthitis, is an affliction of the middle ear that often reduces the sufferer to a stupefied or panic-stricken condition. If he moves his head or eyes, the world about him blurs and spins. If he gets to his feet, the floor quakes, tilts, and falls away, while the walls and ceiling slant at eccentric angles. If he walks outside, the houses sway and topple, and the pavement races towards him underfoot like an advancing wave, bearing on its crest the reeling, distorted forms of advancing pedestrians. His own body seems to undergo fantastic changes, the limbs extending to giant size at one moment, and contracting into stubs the next. Like the intellectuals of Laputa, the sufferer inhabits neither heaven nor earth: his home is a "Floating Island" in mid-air round which the horizon wheels and tilts with nauseating violence. For a full account of this horrible state of "gravitational anarchy", which often kept Swift shut helplessly in the Deanery for days on end, see the article: "Impression: Essentially Normal", by Berton Roueché (*The New Yorker*, April 5, 1958).

increase proportionately as his expectations diminish; his government of his little kingdom becomes the more despotic as the last chances of escaping from it fade away. The less power he has in large matters, the more furiously he exercises it in small ones, becoming more a terror than a friend to his courtiers and intimates. No longer in a position to guide ministers of state, he imposes absolute guidance upon lesser people—and this he does, most characteristically, not as an abuse of power but as a public duty. "Corrigible people are to be chid", he informs one of the ladies of his little court in a brusque note, adding: "those who are otherwise may be safe from any lectures of mine". This corollary should be noted, because even in his harshest years, Swift acted according to the rules. Those who came to him for correction received it, but they were under no obligation to come. The Chapter that supported his edicts with unanimity and the merchant bodies that obeyed his orders absolutely were composed of free men who gave their allegiance to Swift because they wished to do so. Such a man may be a terror, but he is not a tyrant.

What slowly dies is the old gaiety, strangled to death by circumstances, wilfullness, chagrin and illness. The Swift we see confined to his deanery for weeks on end, stricken with the nausea and vertigo of his disease; or running furiously up and down the stairs on days when it is too wet for him to ride, becomes, without gaiety, a "wild Dean" indeed and an eccentric of marked degree. Sitting below his cherished portrait of Charles I, he is inflamed by the most trifling examples of a contemporary degeneracy, and maddened in his last years as if it were only yesterday, when he reads in a magazine of how "My grandfather was so persecuted and plundered two and fifty times by the barbarity of Cromwell's hellish crew", obliging "the poor old gentleman to sell the better half of his estate to support the family". Born, he insists, "to a million disappointments", he is condemned to re-enact

"in miniature" the great days of his past, ruling a realm
of "a hundred and twenty houses, whose inhabitants constitute the bulk of my subjects": the effect is to see his
"present life as the exact burlesque of my middle age".

But the marvel is that the gaiety struggles to survive
to the very end, not only in despite of circumstance but
in despite of Swift himself. For as the years pass, much
of Swift's pleasure is obtained from the pursuit of grimness, and becomes a self-punitive exercise, or a gigantic
tantrum, in which the fixed determination to refuse consolation is always mixed with an impassioned need for it.
Good-hearted, witty men like Gay and Arbuthnot can
supply this consolation; but when they die, memories of
their mistreatment well up and bring indignation to the
boil again. A brave, clever young woman like the Duchess of Queensberry can boldly ignore the terrible Dean
and appeal in her admirable letters to the humorous
affectionate Doctor, but in the end she is almost alone as
an artist of captivation; the remaining women in Swift's
life are mere pupillary serfs, fit only to be lectured,
bullied and pinched. To see life in terms of a farce, in
which "fools only are serious", as Lord Bathurst suggests
to Swift, becomes impossible: life is *not* a farce, Swift
declares: it is "a ridiculous tragedy, which is the worst
kind of composition". The only consolation for this detestable condition is to be found in religious faith, and
what this enjoins upon the elderly is laid down with
awful clarity by Swift in a letter to a bereaved mother:

> God, in his wisdom, hath been pleased to load our declining
> years with many sufferings, with diseases, and decays of
> nature, with the death of many friends, and the ingratitude
> of more, sometimes with the loss or diminution of our for-
> tunes, when our infirmities most need them; often with con-
> tempt from the world, and always with neglect from it, with
> the death of our most hopeful or useful children, with a want
> of relish for all worldly enjoyments, with a general dislike of

persons and things, and though all these are very natural effects of increasing years, yet they were intended by the author of our being to wean us gradually from our fondness of life, the nearer we approach towards the end of it. And this is the use you are to make in prudence, as well as in conscience, of all the afflictions you have hitherto undergone, as well as of those which in the course of nature and providence you have reason to expect.

In the absolute finality of this we see, in highly illustrative form, the essence of the will-power that made greatness and wretchedness *necessary* portions of Swift's life. We realize that he imposes on everything that comes his way, from deity to trifles, a fixed shape or nature that must always remain unalterable. He gives to the whole history of mankind and to all events a theme or personal interpretation that is wholly his own: where this interpretation is refuted by evidence, he always rejects the latter in order to maintain the former. If he does not forgive Mrs. Howard, it is because to do so would mean changing the shape he has imposed forever upon the events with which she is concerned; if, on the other hand, he can forget having written *The Windsor Prophecy* or utterly ignore the vices of such as Henry St. John and Lady Masham, this is again because such forgetfulness and blindness are essential to the picture he had drawn of Queen Anne's last years. It may seem incredible to us that he believed Charles I to be a paragon among kings—until we realize that to correct such a belief would involve destroying absolutely the whole conception of English history on which his attitudes were based. In the last analysis all facts were subject to Swift's power of fiction: he could see the world only in imaginative shapes of his own making. Nietzsche sums up this sort of man very nicely when he says: "A sign of strong character, when once the resolution has been taken, to shut the ear even to the best counter-arguments. Occasionally, therefore, a will to stupidity". And not only occasionally but always, one may add, a will to bitter and inevitable disappointment.

❋   ❋   ❋

Nearly all the poems that we find so horrifying today were written in this last period of disappointment. But so was the multitude of trivial ones that shocked dignified people like Orrery just as much—the jingles and doggerels, the excellent riddles in verse form, the "cries" of Dublin pedlars:

> Charming Oysters I cry . . .
>
> Ripe 'Sparagrass,
> Fit for lad or lass . . .

and the cheerful pursuits of ingenious rhymes that Byron admired so much, saying: "Swift beats us all hollow when it comes to rhymes". In fact, Byron carried the game to its highest perfection in *Don Juan*, but the master was not too far behind his pupil:

> But as for me, who ne'er could clamber high,
> To understand Malebranche or Cambray;
> Who send my mind (as I believe) less
> Than others do, on errands sleeveless . . .
> Am more diverted with a quibble
> Than dreams of worlds intelligible;
> And think all notions too abstracted
> Are like the ravings of a crackt head. . . .

It is part of the charm of these "minor" poems that so many of them are neat, exact reflections of the author's character, resolves and prejudices. Here are the farewells to hope, briskly expressed:

> I am, as now too late I find,
> The greatest cully of mankind . . .

the firm, but never effective, resolve to bring to a stop:

Those thankless and officious cares
I use to take in friends affairs
From which I never could refrain
And have been often chid in vain . . .

here, indeed, are every aspect of Swift's character from the sharpest spite to the highest delight. The short form suits his talents very well, for a long poem often asks too much of him and tends to expire slowly after a brisk start. A notable exception is *The Grand Question Debated*, in which an Irish maidservant describes to her mistress, first, the formal visit to the master of the house of a Captain of Horse, and second, the same Captain's reappearance the following day to pay his respects with all his troop. Here is the formal visit:

Now, see, when they meet, how their Honour's behave;
Noble CAPTAIN, your Servant—Sir ARTHUR your slave;
You honour me much—the Honour is mine,—
'Twas a sad rainy Night—but the Morning is fine—
Pray, how does my Lady?—My Wife's at your Service.—
I think I have seen her Picture by JERVIS.—
Good Morrow, good Captain,—I'll wait on you down,—
You shan't stir a Foot— You'll think me a Clown—
For all the World, CAPTAIN, not half an Inch farther—
You must be obey'd—your Servant, Sir ARTHUR;
My humble Respects to my Lady unknown,—
I hope you will use my House as your own.

and here the Captain's arrival with all his troop to pay their respects to Sir Arthur's lady:

Next day, to be sure, the CAPTAIN will come,
At the Head of his Troop, with Trumpet and Drum:
Now, Madam, observe, how he marches in State:—
The Man with the Kettle-drum enters the Gate;
DUB, DUB, A-DUB, DUB. The Trumpeters follow,
TANTARA, TANTARA, while all the Boys hollow.
See, now comes the Captain all dawb'd with gold lace:
O law! the sweet Gentleman! look in his Face;

And see how he rides like a Lord of the Land,
With the fine flaming Sword that he holds in his Hand;
And his Horse, the dear CRETER, it prances and rears,
With Ribbins in Knots, at its Tail and its Ears;
At last comes the Troop, by Word of Command
Drawn up in our Court; when the Captain cries, *STAND.*
Your LADYSHIP lifts up the Sash to be seen,
(For sure, I had DIZEN'D you out like a QUEEN.)
The CAPTAIN, to shew he is proud of the Favour,
Looks up to your Window, and cocks up his Beaver.
(His Beaver is cock'd; pray, Madam, mark that,
For, a CAPTAIN of Horse never takes off his Hat;
Because he has never a Hand that is idle;
For, the Right holds the Sword, and the Left holds
  the Bridle.)
Then flourishes thrice his Sword in the Air,
As a compliment due to a Lady so fair;
How I tremble to think of the Blood it has spilt!
Then he low'rs down the Point, and kisses the Hilt.
Your LADYSHIP smiles, and thus you begin;
Pray, CAPTAIN, be pleas'd to light, and walk in:
The CAPTAIN salutes you with Congee profound;
And your LADYSHIP curchyes half way to the Ground!

This is the "merry" Swift that was well known to his friends and is too often neglected by those who write about him now. It is prominent among the amiable characteristics that must be reckoned with before we accept the "amazing madman" posited by Mr. T. S. Eliot, the human beast imagined by Sir Harold Nicolson, the villifier of mankind seen by George Orwell. If such summations were correct, Swift's would be one of the simplest characters that ever existed and one would be obliged to wonder how he managed to go so far with such limited capacities. Nor should we find him so irresistible and return again and again, in every generation, to examine the riddles and puzzles that he passed down to us as his last will and testament.

❖   ❖   ❖

Swift's life is both a triumph of personal ambition and an absolute public failure. The intensity of his disappointments can be judged by the fact that though his literary genius was never in doubt, the opinions he expressed with it, on major matters, were always ineffective and almost uninfluential. The life we live today descends in a direct line from his doughty opposite, Defoe; all that Swift's eminence does is let us see, stamped clearly on his great figure, the principles and politics from which we have completely departed. Given the backward inclination that inspired it, it is a life that spans almost exactly a century, from the final defeat of the Cavaliers in 1645 to the last Jacobite rebellion of 1745—from Clarendon's principles to Walpole's. A way of thought that was old-fashioned even in the thinker's lifetime has so entirely vanished now that we are not only wholly out of sympathy with it but find it barely comprehensible. To love and admire Swift is a whimsical act, for he has no body of followers in his opinions and is as much a scandal to the modern Tory as he is unacceptable to the Radical libertarian. His only example is that of prescience, in that the changes he opposed so ineffectively have all come to pass, usually in the way in which he foretold they would. It was clear to him, to cite a small example, that without strict regulation the English language would become an immense grab-bag of casual forms and expressions: none would deny that it has done so.

It was equally clear to him that a national economy rooted in banks and stocks instead of land would change the whole order of existence: today, we so take this change for granted that we think Swift must have been unbalanced to regard a national bank as the gigantic swindle of dishonourable "projectors". In both these matters we do, however, pause occasionally to consider his point of view and even to recognize its merits.

We have even better reason to do this in matters of religion and ethics, in both of which Swift's opinions are

both prophetic and intolerable. It was his firm belief
that the Church of his day must move backwards, his-
torically speaking: were it to move with the times, the
times would eventually get rid of it. A tolerant Church
of England, Swift insisted, could not do the duty of an
Established Church: immunity from competition was
essential to its existence. Consistently with this belief in
a single religion, he denied the right of Deists and Pres-
byters to throw doubts on it in published books, arguing
that once sufferance was granted to such rebels, free-
thinking and atheism would soon follow them into print.
Finally, he denied the right of the clergyman to propound
rational explanations of the miraculous, arguing that
such well-intended efforts to explain the inexplicable
must ultimately destroy the basis of faith on which
Christianity stood.

In all these matters he has been proved right. The
British nation, favouring freedom of worship over an
Established Church, now lives with a Church that is still
Established but has virtually ceased to be a church. The
fifty churches that Swift persuaded Queen Anne to build
in order to accommodate a few hundred thousand Lon-
doners are now far too numerous to accommodate some
millions. The rational base of Christianity is become one
of the few necessary articles of faith, and what the atheist
has failed to shake, the "Broad" divine has gladly up-
rooted. Most of us are well satisfied with this state of
affairs and cannot fail to resent any efforts that are made
by this peculiar Church to inspire us with belief in
Christian revelation. What has been abandoned by the
devout can never be attractive to the atheist.

Swift's attitude to Church matters is not likely to be
commended today, except by Roman Catholics. But one
must admire his prescience in foretelling the event so
accurately—and perhaps add, as final evidence of his
religious faith, that though he foresaw the death of the
Church, he could not believe to his dying day that this

death would invalidate its claims: simply by having lived, he declared, it would justify the prophecy that "the gates of Hell shall not prevail against it". What he did not foresee, of course, was that these gates would become mere allegorical entries to an allegorical place and, as such, perfectly acceptable to every progressive "projector" in the physical sciences.

The political failure is no less pronounced than the religious one. Swift's ideal of a government above "faction" was bound to follow the Church of England into oblivion, because the two were interdependent in his view: he conjoined his religion and his politics by believing, as Murry says, that "The full citizen of England must be a professed member of the Church of England." This denying of the franchise to those outside the Church makes his idea of a politics that is above faction impure and unacceptable, because it is, itself, a basically factional opinion that insists that the reasonable man can only be regarded as such if his religious views are the same as Swift's. History has not merely dismissed this point of view as exorbitant and unjust but has gone to the other extreme in denying it. What Trevelyan has called "the genius of the British people" has established faction as the very model of democratic government: indeed, this "genius" has been so generally approved that there can be no harm in asking whether it deserves so noble a title. If faction were to give place to government by those best fitted to perform it, this would show a spirit and intelligence entirely worthy to be called "genius", because it would express both an extraordinary wisdom on the part of the voters and a high capacity for unselfishness in the politicians. But we get no such impression from the workings of our present Parliamentary system, because where faction is obligatory, wisdom and unselfishness must always be relatively unimportant. Indeed, once it becomes the duty of one party to deny what the other party affirms, government assumes a reality of high comedy that must be disguised by appearances of deep solemnity. Words like *genius* are an important part of this necessary disguise, and by faith in the unreal word we exorcise the real comedy. The standard demanded by Swift is an improper one because it is unjust, but the ideal to which it aspires cannot be dismissed as old-fashioned and undemocratic merely because we like to believe that genius and faction are synonymous. Honesty, competence and intelligence replace Party as our standard as soon as our liberties are endangered by another power: perhaps the strain of maintaining so rational a standard of government in wartime is why we dedicate the long periods of peace to the refreshments of farce.

Finally, there is the matter of liberty, which is the most interesting of all in regard to Swift because all his opinions on all subjects—language, behaviour, politics, human rights, conversation—stand together in the end under this one head and show us vividly the extensive unity obtained by his single-mindedness. We know how much he cherished liberty:

> Fair Liberty was all his cry
> For her, he was prepared to die . . .

but only if we are ignorant of his real character and life do we suppose that the "liberty" of which he spoke had any resemblance to the liberty we adore today. Swift's liberty is a sort of despotism by today's standards: we only delude ourselves if we picture the Irish patriot as a spokesman for our own kind of freedom. Swift regards all liberty as an arrangement of severe disciplines: these are binding upon all persons from the king himself down to the lowest subject. The daughter must be absolutely obedient to the mother; the monarch to the constitutional law; the servant to the master; the conversation to the social rule; the poem to the settled form. Freedom of speech is the prerogative of government by law established: it can be neither enjoyed nor demanded by the opposing minority so long as the powerful majority keeps its actions within constitutional bounds. Freedom of belief comes under the same head: it may exist, but only because it cannot be eradicated, and it should never be translated into freedom of worship. The man who holds constitutional power may employ authors to present his case and attack his enemies; but should these enemies retaliate in kind, their statements must be regarded as "libels" and their attitude condemned as illegal and anarchistic.

This is the point of view that has been described as *romanitas*—the old European view that discipline and law themselves bespeak liberty, which is only chaos and anarchy without them and cannot be tolerated, let alone desired and idolized, as a separate ideal. When king and government usurp the law in Ireland, they step at once beyond the pale of legal right: they are open to attack by the Dean in the name of liberty because they have substituted personal whims for established practices. The libertarian Dean is fighting, in essence, not as a rebel against the established order but as its spokesman. He enjoins upon those who follow his banner the absolute obedience that he himself would pay to a king and government that remained obedient to the laws.

Today, when the personal act and opinion suggest liberty and the established order its curtailment, Swift's point of view seems more a denial of freedom than an assent to it. It is, in fact, simply an order of things that is becoming more unfamiliar to us all the time, and this particularly in a century when we scarcely dare to distinguish between the law and order demanded by Swift and the despotism of modern dictators. And yet we should be brave enough to try and make this distinction because Swift's view has something to teach us: we cannot imagine embracing it, but we can use it, at least, as a standpoint from which to see our own forms of liberty with a more critical eye. We are, for example, thankful that we shall never be stood in the pillory for printing attacks upon our lawful government, but this need not cause us to insist too much that the principal aim and function of our newspapers, at present, is the defence of our liberty and the sweetness of our society. If we declare our joy at having rid ourselves of the injustices of *romanitas*, we must at least also show our contempt for those who have profited so richly by its absence; if we insist that Grub Street, like faction, is the very soil of liberty, we must still feel something of the horror that Swift would have felt at seeing it become an avenue of shady peerages.

Our quarrel with Swift is ultimately a quarrel with his peculiar character. In spite of all the horrible barbarities of our own age, we still refuse to accept an attitude to life that recognizes only two extremes—perfect brutishness and perfect reasonableness. We recognize that these were the extremes of his own nature and that much of his personal life was spent in trying to impose the inflexible reasonableness of a Houyhnhnm upon the savagery of a Yahoo. His own nature was his mirror of mankind, and the absolute authority that his own fury demanded is the authority that he attempted to impose upon the world. He knew that the Yahoo in him was an animal of abnormal strength and wildness:

> And, when indecently I rave,
> When out my brutish passions break,
> With gall in ev'ry word I speak . . .

he could suggest only one way of controlling it, an intellectual rigour of equal hardness. These extremities of passion and discipline are so far beyond the compass of the majority of persons that they start back in some horror when they read of a life that was lived to a large extent on a scale of struggle that they find hardly imaginable. Fortunately, it can always be seen that a struggle that was too extreme for life was admirably suited to the art of writing. It is the imposition of an absolute authority upon the most violent of passions that gives Swift's best works the directed vigour and bridled energy beside which the works of more middling sort of men seem clumsy, faint and insipid.

We think of the centaur when we consider Swift's works, or of Plato's charioteer and horses. Swift may have done so himself but have thought it would be a more vexatious truth to reverse the accepted model and show the horse as the governing philosopher and man as the incorrigible brute. This excellent fancy was a simple one to execute: it ran into danger only when the ironist stopped to reflect that the perfect reasonableness of the Houyhnhnms might suggest to the warlike Yahoo a frailty and incapacity for self-defence of which brutish advantage might be taken. Such a supposition required squashing and received it in the famous passage:

Imagine twenty thousand of them breaking into the midst of an European army, confounding the ranks, overturning the carriages, battering the warriors' faces into mummy by terrible yerks from their hinder hoofs; they would well deserve the character given to Augustus, *Recalcitrat undique tutus.*

Not the voice of reason, but the trumpet of the Cavalier.

❄❄❄❄❄ INDEX ❄❄❄❄❄